# The Friendship Book

## A THOUGHT FOR EACH DAY | 2018

# The Friendship Book

*THE past is another country,*
*We don't live there any more,*
*We left it all behind us,*
*New pathways to explore.*
*So forward now, with lighter heart*
*We'll walk with firmer tread,*
*And see that bright horizon –*
*It's shining up ahead!*

*The past has lessons we must learn,*
*They helped to make us strong.*
*They nurtured many hopes and dreams,*
*Placed in our hearts a song.*
*Tomorrow's waiting out of sight,*
*Who knows what's on the way?*
*The future beckons you and me,*
*Farewell to yesterday!*

– Iris Hesselden.

# January

THE line "Who would true valour see" comes from the hymn popularly known as "To Be A Pilgrim", but it is also associated with the Anderson family.

It might seem at first that all the valour was Sheila's. She married Ian already knowing that he would be paralysed for the rest of his life. What a courageous woman!

But what of Ian's story? How did he come to be paralysed? Ian was part of a volunteer RAF regiment during World War II and his plane went down in 1942. Now, that was courage! Not to mention the spirit it took to adapt to a normal life afterwards.

A man's courage and a woman's courage might often express themselves in very different ways. And, sometimes, as with the Anderson family, two heroes (neither of whom would call themselves that) find each other.

Who would true valour see? Look around you. Sometimes you need look no further than your neighbours, or your family.

NOT every American tradition transfers – or should transfer – across the Atlantic to Britain. But I rather like the idea they have in some of their calendars of calling January National Thank-you Month.

In a time of year that is traditionally rather bleak, finding something to be thankful for each day throughout January will not only remind us of our blessings, it might even give the impression of spring coming early.

And I am thankful for anything that does that!

## Wednesday — January 3

*THERE'S happiness in simple things:*
*A rosebud drenched in dew;*
*The letter that the postman brings;*
*A baby's smile for you!*

*The calling bird at early dawn;*
*Rainbow's pastel light;*
*A field of gently waving corn;*
*The sunset's flame at night.*

*There's happiness in simple things,*
*They're part of every day;*
*So cherish them within your heart*
*To help you on your way.*

– Elizabeth Gozney.

## Thursday — January 4

THESE words are supposedly taken from a bishop's tomb in the crypts of Westminster Abbey. It has been a while since I went searching any crypts, so I can't personally vouch for that, but I can vouch for their powerful truth.

"When I was young and free and my imagination had no limits, I dreamed of changing the world. As I grew older and wiser, I discovered that the world would not change, so I lowered my sights somewhat and decided to change only my country. But it, too, seemed immovable.

"As I grew into my twilight years, in one last desperate attempt, I settled for changing only my family, those closest to me, but alas, they would have none of it.

"And now as I lie on my deathbed, I suddenly realise: if only I had changed myself first, then by example I would have changed my family. From their inspiration and encouragement, I would then have been able to better my country and, who knows, I may have even changed the world."

Snowy reflections.

Rannoch Moor, Scotland.

## Friday — January 5

IN Lamlash, on the beautiful Isle of Arran, a row of cottages looks out across the bay. Once upon a time these were the homes of fishing folk. They all look pretty much the same – except for the dormer windows protruding from the long roof.

A sharp-eyed observer might notice that the topmost window in each cottage has a distinctly different pattern of panes. One has a single pane of glass, another two panes, another three, four, six, eight, and so on.

The idea was that the fisherman's wife would leave a lamp in the window and the fisherman, returning home in the dark after a long day at sea, would recognise his own house from a mile off and know someone there was thinking of him.

You might think one love is pretty much like another, but those who are in it know that no matter how similar their love looks to every other love, there is really nothing in the world exactly like it.

The windows in the fishermen's cottages remind us that even though love might be universal, it is also endlessly individual and unique.

## Saturday — January 6

CLYRO in Wales is a popular holiday destination and a beautiful town in its own right. Back in the 1870s the local minister recorded much of the life of the village in his diary.

I particularly like the account of the time he was caught unawares by the place he lived in.

"The beauty of the first view of the village this evening was indescribable. The brilliant golden poplar spire shone in the evening light . . . and the blossoming fruit trees blazed with a transparent green and white lustre in the setting sunlight. The village is a blaze of fruit blossoms. Clyro at its loveliest. What more can be said?"

If we are lucky enough to stumble on such an entrancing moment, either in our home town or in some place we might be visiting, then there really is only one more thing to say.

Thank you!

IN the 1720s Hans Egede went to Greenland as a young missionary. He wasn't very successful.

He didn't speak the local language and people showed no interest in his Bible readings, or his stories about Jesus.

Then a smallpox epidemic swept the island. Hundreds, including Egede's wife, died.

As he worked to help those remaining, they saw that he shared in their grief, saw that he was part of the community in his efforts to help . . . and they started listening to his sermons.

Jesus didn't preach from on high. He never separated himself from the people he wanted to help. He walked among them. He lived as one of them.

Whether you want to spread the Gospel, help someone, or simply get on with others, you should walk with them a while, share in their highs and lows.

When they come to know that you are no different in the essentials, then they will be interested in the extra you have to offer.

ANDY teaches a Sunday school class. He asked the children how many words they could think of that that included the word "love." They came up with loving, loved, beloved . . . Then one little lad suggested loveful.

Andy explained that he didn't think it was a real word, but the lad wasn't convinced.

"We can be sorrowful, or joyful, or hateful. Why can't we be loveful?"

Andy did some research and discovered that the word actually was in everyday use in the 13th century, but since then it has fallen out of popularity – and out of many dictionaries.

So, he set the class the same challenge I am passing on to you. Live your life in such a way that "loveful" is the only way to describe it, and let's bring the word back!

## Tuesday — January 9

I'S a verse from the ancient Sanskrit. No-one knows who the writer was, but we can still apply the words to modern life.

"Look at this day," it says. "In it lie all the realities and truths of existence; the bliss of growth, the splendour of action; the glory of power . . ."

In other words, that ancient writer is reminding us that each day has all the possibilities of every day, if we appreciate that! If we go into the New Year with that thought in mind, how exciting will the year ahead seem – and be?

## Wednesday — January 10

THE poet and author Fritz Reuter was heading towards a legal career when membership of a student political group saw him arrested and sentenced to death.

He was eventually pardoned, but his career prospects were wiped out. Making his living as a writer, he penned these thoughts. They might have been influenced by his own experiences and tell us a lot about the man himself.

"Nobody's life flows on such an even course that it does not sometimes come up against a dam and swirl round and round. Something happens to everyone. He or she must take care the water of their life stays clear, and that heaven and earth are reflected in it."

## Thursday — January 11

WOULD you like to be able to work miracles?

When slavery was an economic and social reality, the idea of ending it must have seemed an impossibility. Back then, Lydia Maria Child, who worked for its abolition, wrote her recipe for success.

"Love," she wrote, "is the divine vitality that everywhere produces and restores life. To each and every one of us, it gives the power of working miracles if we will."

Will we?

A stunning view.

*Posforth Gill waterfall, Yorkshire.*

## Friday — January 12

MEDICAL science continues to come up with ever more wonderful remedies. There is a spectacular array of treatments, but the one thing they have in common – those that work – is that they heal the patient, but have no effect on the doctor, or the nurse, dispensing them.

Doctor Karl Menninger's field was psychiatry rather than physical health, but he did claim to have found at least one two-way treatment.

"Love cures people," he said, "the ones who receive the love, and the ones who give it, too."

## Saturday — January 13

IN 1855 Wilson Bentley photographed a snowflake. He went on to photograph over 5,000 more and not one of them was the same as any other. Each was beautiful in its own way.

So, how can we ever say we are bored? If there is such wondrous variety in something as ephemeral as a snowflake, then where could we not look and be fascinated, if we look close enough?

## Sunday — January 14

IHAVE never understood American football, but I do appreciate this secret of success shared by one of its coaches. It was, "Three yards and a cloud of dust."

In other words, if every time his players got the ball they covered three yards in the right direction before the other team jumped on them, then they would get there. It wouldn't be showy or spectacular, but, three yards at a time, they would reach the touchdown line.

It might seem like life is always stopping you from getting where you want to go, but if you pick yourself up each time and gain another three yards before the next cloud of dust descends – you will get there in the end!

---

THOMAS À KEMPIS was talking about love in its completeness; about the love between mankind and God, God and mankind. But he might just as easily have been talking about the love of a parent for a child, an adult for an aged friend, a lover for a partner in distress . . . He described it thus:

"Love is ever on the watch; it rests but it does not slumber, it is wearied but not spent, alarmed but not dismayed."

Have you had that sort of love in your life? Have you given that sort of love? Then you surely have shared in something divine.

---

REFERRING to times of trouble and tragedy, Billy Graham said, "Times like this will do one of two things: they will either make us hard and bitter and angry at God, or they will make us tender and open, and help us reach out in trust and faith."

If you're not interested in God or faith you can substitute love and life. But the choice remains the same and no-one else makes it for us. So . . . given that there is no life without trouble, which will you choose?

---

OUR dear friend Mary has some younger friends who, recently, seem to have stumbled from one difficult time to another. Having pity on them for their youth, I said, "It's a good thing they have a wise friend like you to keep them right."

"Wise, is it?" she replied with a laugh. She thought for a moment, then said, "If I have anything approaching wisdom it has come from surviving times like they are growing through. And I had help, too."

I retracted my sympathy after that. The difficult times weren't burdens being inflicted on Mary's young friends. They were really the seeds of future wisdom and understanding, for the time when they, in their turn, would be helpers.

## Thursday — January 18

IT'S usually a pleasant thing, especially on a cold, dark night, to arrive at a house and see a light shining from behind the curtains. It means someone is in and you can probably expect a welcome.

An anonymous sage drew a similar conclusion about something quite different.

"A smile," he said, "is the lighting system of the face and the heating system of the heart."

So, when you see one, you know someone is at home, and you'll find a warm welcome there, too!

## Friday — January 19

HOW would you like to be an artist? Ah, but I can't paint, I hear some of you say. It doesn't matter, is my reply!

Ray Kroc developed the worldwide McDonald's fast-food franchise from one outlet and a few ideas. He later said, "The French fry is my canvas."

Now, I don't imagine anyone would call chips high art, but it does remind me that any one of us can take what we do, and do it artistically!

## Saturday — January 20

PROFESSOR GILBERT MURRAY, Australian-born philosopher, linguist and the leading expert on classical Greek culture in his day, lived a fascinating life. Many are the quotes I could select of his.

But the one that tells us most about the man comes from a comment made in 1933 (when Murray was sixty-seven) about a hero of his who had just died.

This man passed away after sliding down a long banister and falling off the end. He was eighty years old! I would guess the unnamed hero and the good professor had a similar take on life – that it should be happily lived!

## Sunday — January 21

*IT sometimes makes me sad to think*
*Of all the years gone by,*
*The folks I've known, the happy days –*
*Oh, dear, how time does fly.*
*But no – I will not be downcast,*
*Nor sit with gloomy brow,*
*Today is mine, and that's enough,*
*I'll prize the Here and Now.*
*For all I have and all I do,*
*Enriches every day,*
*I'll take each moment as it comes,*
*Rejoicing on my way!*

– Maggie Ingall.

## Monday — January 22

WHEN the money is spent, it's gone. When the film is over it is, as the French say, *fini*. When the sun sets we cannot raise it back up. Some things just end.

But when a man or a woman can't stand any more of someone's nonsense, when they run out of patience, when they simply cannot walk another step, or give another chance, or love again – they can! If they want to enough. The most wonderful things in life endure, and have no end.

## Tuesday — January 23

THE Italians have a philosophy called *La Bella Figura*; the Beautiful Figure. It means many things, like dressing to impress and living as if you are always on show. It also means doing the little things in life beautifully.

And when you think about it, why would we want to fill our lives with anything other than elegance and beauty?

And, of course, we are always on show. But thankfully the One who does see everything we do sees beauty in all its guises.

## Wednesday — January 24

JANUARY gets its name from the Roman god Janus. He had two faces, one looking into the past, the other looking forward, into the future. At least he wouldn't get a sore neck from turning round all the time!

The past is a lovely place to visit, but all too often, people get stuck there or prefer to stay there because they don't think there is much to look forward to. Can I suggest we do visit the past, the good and the bad, in order to learn from it, and be better equipped to make a future worth looking forward to?

This January, let us spend a while contemplating the last twelve months. And then set about recreating them, or improving on them, in the year ahead.

## Thursday — January 25

ONE great Scottish writer, Robert Louis Stevenson, wrote of another, Robert Burns, "To write with authority about another man we must have fellow-feeling and some common ground of experience with our subject." That very trait was, perhaps, what raised Robert Burns above the average scribbler – his ability to find fellow feeling with people from all parts of society.

Surely that understanding – one we might all work on – is the philosophy behind some of Burns's most famous words. "A man's a man for a' that."

## Friday — January 26

HOW is this year's crop doing?" I asked Harry when someone mentioned New Year's resolutions.

"Oh, I haven't made any new resolutions since 1978," he told me. "I made some good ones that year. And I'm still working on them!"

Too often we focus on the smaller issues in life. And if something changes things for the better then it should be worth working on for the rest of our lives.

*HE'S full of love, he's faithful,*
*Almost everything we share.*
*Though sometimes he's a handful,*
*I'm lost if he's not there.*
*He is part of my family, So I never am alone,*
*I'll treasure him, for in this life,*
*From God he is on loan.*
*When it's his time to leave me,*
*I'll not grieve and think he's gone,*
*Our loving link's eternal,*
*I'll know my pet lives on.*
*For in his doggy heaven,*
*He will wait, whole, free from pain;*
*Think how he'll race to meet me*
*On the day we meet again!*

*– Chrissy Greenslade.*

WHO doesn't enjoy seeing, in person or on film, whales as they surface, spout majestically and bring their tails splashing down? Their size and sheer presence leave most people in awe.

Those visits to the surface, and contacts with humans, are probably a novelty for the whales as well. You see, they spend the vast majority of their lives feeding and travelling at great depths. To them, home is deep beneath the surfaces of the world's oceans.

And yet, they couldn't stay down there for ever. They still need to come to the surface from time to time, simply to breathe.

Without contact with that strange upper realm, which is so different from the environment they are most comfortable with, they would die.

We're not so dissimilar. We spend most of our time in one world, this earth with all its comforts and all its problems, but it is the contact with the upper realm that makes this journey worthwhile and reminds us that the stuff of life really is "up there"!

## Monday — January 29

THE future can be a scary place. Many of us will lose sleep worrying over what might happen there. But the philosopher and writer Ralph Waldo Emerson, who lived in the 19th century, offered the present advice from the past on how to handle the future.

"Don't waste time in doubts and fears," he wrote. "Spend yourself on the work before you, well assured that the right performance of this hour's duties will be the best preparation for the hours and ages that follow it."

Do "now" the best you can and "later" will be built on a better foundation.

## Tuesday — January 30

HOW are your New Year Resolutions faring? Well, I hope. I wish I could say the same about mine.

The Lady of the House (who assures me she can occasionally be less than perfect, although I can scarcely believe it) shared her secret to successfully giving up bad habits.

"It's not just about moving the negative things out of your life," she explained. "That still leaves a space for them to come back to. You also have to fill those spaces with good things so there is nowhere for those old habits to come back to."

Filling your life with so many good things that there is no space for the bad? How does that sound for a late resolution, or as a boost for the ones already made?

## Wednesday — January 31

DID you hear about the poor man who had everything? If you did, would you sympathise with him? Would you think him a poor man? I would. You see, having everything meant he had nothing to strive for, nothing to look forward to, nothing left to achieve.

I don't know about you, but as someone who has a bit less than everything I still feel like the much richer man!

An expanse of blue.

Cliffs Of Moher, Ireland

# February

## Thursday — February 1

To my credit, I didn't end up flat on my back. But when I did lose my footing on the ice, my arms and legs went everywhere, spinning in directions I didn't know they could go, before I regained my balance.

I restored my footing and thought I had kept my dignity intact, until I realised that our dear friend Mary had seen me. She let me off lightly, though.

"Well done, Francis!" she shouted from the other side of the road. "Some people fall and let it stop them. Others turn it into a part of their dance. And that was a beautiful dance!"

I am sure she was sharing a philosophical truth with me – but I'd be on slippery ground if I insisted she wasn't also having fun at my expense.

## Friday — February 2

It was one of the coldest spells I can remember and he came looking for bedcovers. He had a flat with a bed in it, but he was using curtains as covers.

Not wanting to risk giving money to someone I hardly knew, I suggested we take a walk together to the local supermarket (which I wasn't even sure sold bedding).

Trying to be subtle, I counted my money while it was still in my pocket, carrying on the conversation all the while. I didn't think I had enough on me to make a difference.

When we arrived at the shop the shelves facing the door had been set up as a Sale area and there, right in front of us, were half-price duvets! At a time when such things should have been at a premium! And the price of one duvet was the same amount I had in my pocket.

Sometimes, you just have to set out in trust. Walk firmly towards the good you want to do . . . and be prepared to be amazed!

## Saturday — February 3

WE should concern ourselves with the thought of an afterlife – but not forget we are in this life for a time and a purpose. Pearl S. Buck, the daughter of missionaries to China, once wrote, "I am so absorbed in the wonder of earth and the life upon it that I cannot think of heaven and angels."

The eternal can, and will, wait while we appreciate this life and all its many and varied wonders.

## Sunday — February 4

TODAY is all about life,
Today is all about living,
It's catching the sunshine and seizing the day
And sometimes forgetting, forgiving.
Today is all about you,
The you that is hidden within,
A time to look forward and nurture your dreams
And let those ambitions begin.
Today is all about love,
To comfort the hurt and the strife,
Reach out to each other, each sister and brother,
It's time now to celebrate life!

– Iris Hesselden.

.

## Monday — February 5

WHEN it was discovered in 1905, the Cullinan diamond was the largest gem of its kind ever found. It may have been the most valuable single item in the world at that time – which made it a big security risk.

When it was sent from South Africa to England it was placed, amidst great ceremony, in a locked box and put into the steamship captain's safe where it was guarded every second of the journey.

Except it wasn't. It was actually posted, in a plain box, via the ordinary mail service. All the rest was a distraction.

I find that God delivers his treasures in a very similar way.

## Tuesday — February 6

A FRIEND who is an experienced diver told me of the few times he had gone so deep (without a torch) that it was impossible to see his hand in front of his face.

"Your sense of direction completely disappears," he said. "It is very disorientating."

So I asked how he knew which way was up.

"I felt for the bubbles," he said.

Though we might never find ourselves in such darkness, we can be left directionless by life. In such situations I recommend you look for that which rises – and follow it.

## Wednesday — February 7

WHY are we here? What's the point of it all? There can't be many who haven't wondered what the purpose of life is.

One friend suggested that the purpose of it all is just to be happy. That seemed too simplistic and superficial for the others, but I wonder . . .

The philosopher and essayist Ralph Waldo Emerson disagreed – and I disagreed with Mr Emerson. Or did I?

He wrote, "The purpose of life is not to be happy. It is to be useful, to be honorable, to be compassionate, to have it make some difference that you lived and lived well."

But Mr Emerson . . . wouldn't all of that make you very happy indeed?

## Thursday — February 8

CAN you play a harp?
There is an old Celtic tradition that suggests we play our lives with a five-stringed harp: the senses of touch, smell, sight, taste and hearing.

Practise, and play them with sensitivity and style, and you can make your life a beautiful melody.

Sheep may safely graze.

*Brecon Beacons, South Wales.*

## Friday — February 9

**S**AD to say, no-one has a perfect life and we spend a lot of time coming to terms with those shortcomings. But here's a suggestion, something we might try. The things we lacked in our lives; the things that may have messed our lives up a little; spiritual, familial, societal lacks that helped make it less than it might have been . . .

Let's bring them into our lives by being them for someone else. That kind of healing love works both ways.

## Saturday — February 10

**I**N amongst a box of old second-hand books I found a personal diary. It had drawings of pirates, Red Indians and footballers on the cover. It was tatty and worn, as it was entitled to be. It was dated 1937.

I have no doubt the day-to-day thoughts of a boy living in the run-up to World War II, and living a lifestyle long gone, would have been fascinating to read, but I didn't need to pry. I already knew as much about the young fellow as I needed to.

Inside the front cover he had written in a neat hand, "Let me make this day worthwhile – for someone else."

I don't have to read his diary to know he lived a good life. In that simple thought he was already halfway there.

## Sunday — February 11

**D**O you say grace at mealtimes? It used to be a more common practice than it is these days and nary a meal passed in some households without the children closing their eyes while Father recited a prayer.

These days mealtimes are often less structured and the prayer before eating isn't used so often. But the "grace", strictly speaking, isn't a prayer. It comes from the Latin word *gratiae* and means "thank you".

Now, which of us can't stop before a meal and say thank you to the One who, ultimately, provides all we have?

## Monday — February 12

**A**NYONE who doubts popular culture has an impact on our children should meet three-year-old Beth. I watched as she prepared to scoot her scooter down a "steep" hill and heard her muttering something. I looked at her mum.

"'Rabbits are brave'," Mum explained. "Peter Rabbit says it on the telly. Now she says it every time she's worried."

Our children are affected by what they see on television. Let's make sure they see good things. And I am sure Beatrix Potter would be delighted at being little Beth's inspiration.

## Tuesday — February 13

**T**HE new minister – who must have had some experience of church politics – announced that from then on the church would be a "no-moan zone". By that he meant that if someone didn't like something and didn't have a better alternative, well, what was the use of complaining? But if someone didn't like something and knew how it could be improved then they should tell him, and it would be!

Either way, no moaning was required.

Does that sound like a philosophy worth expanding into other aspects of life?

## Wednesday — February 14

*M*AY *your path lead on to sunlight,*
*Bright flowers line the road,*
*And guardian angels walk with you*
*To lighten every load.*
*May those you love find happiness*
*To warm and lift their hearts,*
*And may they find the joy in life*
*That only love imparts.*
*May every far horizon be filled with hope for you*
*And as the shadows fall away may all your dreams come true.*

*– Iris Hesselden.*

New friends.

## Thursday — February 15

WE'VE all heard the expression "the weakest link". Anne Robinson famously used to dismiss people from her quiz show with the words, "You are the weakest link. Goodbye!"

There is an old Jewish proverb that presents the image slightly differently. Rather than being dismissive of weakness, it points out that "the whole chain fails if the weakest link breaks."

What use are all those good, strong links if one gives way? The unbroken parts will end up in the scrap-heap as well.

In looking after the weakest link we become stronger as a whole.

## Friday — February 16

GOLDEN CAP on the Dorset coast is National Trust land, partly because it has become home to a wonderful array of wild animals and birds. While the Trust protects the area, it had nothing to do with what made it so attractive to wildlife.

That happy aspect came about through the cliffs themselves being prone to regular collapses. They grew too dangerous for humans to venture on to and thus became a safe haven for deer, badgers, sea-birds, birds of prey, foxes and many other species.

Any sort of collapse, in the landscape or in our lives, seems like a terrible thing at the time. But sometimes, with a longer view, it is little more than a rearranging; laying the ground for better to come.

## Saturday — February 17

WHAT do you do when the chance presents itself to get one over on your enemy? According to Dr Martin Luther King Jnr, that is exactly the time "You must not do it."

Did a beaten enemy ever become anything more than resentful, sullen, rebellious, biding their time until they could become a proper enemy again?

But someone who knows you had a chance to beat them – and you chose not to? They have all the makings of a future friend.

## Sunday — February 18

**NORMALLY** believe and proclaim that today is by far the most important day of our lives. After all, it is when we get everything done. It is the one we live in. But who am I to argue with Hollywood legend John Wayne about that? He does make a very good point.

The Duke once said, "Tomorrow is the most important thing in life. It comes to us at midnight, very clean. It's perfect when it arrives, and it puts itself in our hands. It hopes we've learned something from yesterday!"

The great American essayist Ralph Waldo Emerson also spoke out in support of tomorrow.

"Tomorrow is a new day," he wrote. "Begin it well and serenely and with too high a spirit to be encumbered with your old nonsense. The day is all that is good and fair. It is too dear, with all its hopes and invitations, to waste a moment of it on yesterdays."

So, there you have it! I claimed priority among days of our lives for today and two Americans claim it for tomorrow. It must be something to do with the clocks changing or, perhaps, with being in different time zones. I'll have my today and they may have their tomorrow when the world turns far enough in that direction. As it surely will.

## Monday — February 19

**THE** hymn-writer and poet Fanny Crosby had an important visitor to her rescue mission in a poor part of New York. She was showing President Polk around the institution when she spotted an old lady who had once worked there as a cleaner. Not having seen her for years and fearing she might not see her again, Ms Crosby excused herself from the President's party.

It was only afterwards that she feared her behaviour might have been seen as very disrespectful. But President Polk put her mind at ease.

"You have done well," he told her. "Kindness, even to those in the humblest capacity, should be our rule of conduct. By this act you have won my esteem."

## Tuesday — February 20

BACK in the 1920s, Theodore Patten wrote a poem which contained the lines, "Some name him great because his eye is always focused far; but, oh, the bluebells sweet he tramples searching for a star!"

Ambition, foresight, planning ahead – all good things. But it is all too easy to forget that heaven is often at our feet this very day.

## Wednesday — February 21

THE poet John Masefield wrote of flowers growing in stony places and kind things done by men with ugly faces.

It reminded me of the time I offered to help a man with a spider-web tattooed across his face. Despite being in pain (or perhaps because of it), he rebuffed me quite rudely and walked away. Then he came back and apologised. He pointed to the tattoo.

"Looking like this," he explained, "you don't get many offers of help. So – thanks!"

Masefield's poem reminds us that kindness and beauty can come from unexpected places. And my experience tells me that the people least likely to receive kindness and beauty are probably the ones who need it most.

## Thursday — February 22

DO you ever wonder why poets never stop putting it in verse, why writers still write about it, why singers endlessly find new ways to sing about it? Is love really an endless source of inspiration?

It would seem to be, and the novelist Jane Austen would seem to agree. In her published letters we find the opinion that, "There are as many forms of love as there are moments in time."

Try it! Who, or what, are you loving right now? And if you can't immediately think of anyone or anything then you might set about remedying that.

If an endless stream of singers and poets can do it, so can we.

## Friday — February 23

HAVE you ever been part of an invincible host? The phrase might conjure up images of an army of angels, or something from "The Lord Of The Rings". But the deaf and blind educator and inspirational speaker Helen Keller once suggested that you, or even I, might be part of such a thing.

What she said was, "Your success and happiness lies in you. Resolve to keep happy, and your joy and you shall form an invincible host against difficulties."

No swords, horses or wings required. Simply resolve to be happy and you will be unbeatable.

## Saturday — February 24

I OFTEN wonder to what extent a person's facial appearance is dictated by their personality. Let's face it; we don't expect someone with serious-looking features to break out in a good chuckle, do we? Which is why it is always doubly delightful when they do. It reminds us of the old saw about not judging a book by its cover, and it also brings to life these words from Victor Hugo.

"Laughter is the sun that drives winter from the human face."

## Sunday — February 25

*HEAVENLY magic is silence,*
*Refreshing as the showery rain,*
*Inviting pleasant thoughts to bloom,*
*Sweet memories to linger again.*
*Soul of silence,*
*Yours is music, lighter, true,*
*Carrying us over calm seas*
*To peaceful shores anew.*
*Where all is little cameos*
*And solitary rest.*
*A world of intermission*
*Of silence, we love best.*

– Dorothy McGregor.

**Old-world charm.**

*Rye, East Sussex.*

## Monday — February 26

DO you pray? Perhaps at mealtimes, or bedtimes? The Gaels of the Scottish highlands and islands in the 1800s had a prayer for lying down, one for sleeping, one for the bed itself; a prayer for the lighting of the fire and the dowsing of it; a prayer for the fishing, for the weaving, and for peat cutting.

In fact, there was scarcely an aspect of their everyday life that did not have its own communion with the One they felt they owed it to.

Those folk are gone now – but they might teach us modern folk a little about appreciation.

## Tuesday — February 27

HELEN KELLER said, "Optimism is the faith that leads to achievement." Whenever I read these words, I think of a small boy I saw attempting to mount a bigger boy's bike.

"Do you think you can ride that?" I asked, wary for his safety.

"Well, I haven't tried," he replied. "So I don't know I can't."

It turned out he could! But without the optimism that led him to give it a go, neither of us would have known the answer to that question.

## Wednesday — February 28

I SAW it in the morning because one shard caught the sunlight and reflected it into the kitchen. It was so bright it surely must be some mystical jewel.

Walking over, I saw it was a broken bottle. But, discarded and shattered as it was, it had created some beauty. The stone it broke on, however, was dull and almost unnoticed.

One was no more or less noble than the other. But one had absorbed much of the light that fell on it, keeping it for itself. The other had taken the same light and thrown it out again in its own unique way.

May we seek to do the latter with the blessings that fall into our lives.

# March

## Thursday — March 1

HARRY pointed up to where his drainpipe met the roof guttering. In a bend at the top of the pipe a robin had built a nest.

"Mrs Robin started there over a week ago," he told me. "The first nest she built slipped and fell to the ground. The second one did likewise. And the third. I don't know which attempt this nest is but, bless her, she kept trying."

I supposed she must have grown more practised and learned from her mistakes.

"That's not it," Harry informed me. "Do you want to know what made the difference? It rained. Heavily. She built this nest with wet and muddy grass and twigs. Because they were softer they filled the space better. Then they dried and stuck. Soon it'll be a cosy home for her chicks."

Well, they do say "into each life a little rain must fall." What they don't tell you is that it can often be a good thing.

## Friday — March 2

THE Mona Lisa can be quite difficult to get close to. Usually the room where she is displayed in the Louvre is packed with tourists wanting to take her photo.

In the same room hangs the Wedding Feast at Cana by Veronese. It is a painting you could spend a day getting lost in, because of its size and its painstaking detail. Despite this, it often barely gets a glance, because of La Giaconda.

There may well be too much beauty in this world for us to pay attention to all of it, but we shouldn't limit our experience by simply admiring the usual suspects. When everyone is looking in one direction, take a moment to look in another. You might be amazed by what you find.

## Saturday — March 3

*THERE is a certain fashion which improves the way you dress,*
*It brightens every style you wear, enhances cheerfulness;*
*You really wouldn't think so but the truth is always there,*
*It has such great importance in the special one you wear.*
*It's never out of date and it will rarely let you down,*
*Can cause a great reaction, change a mood, remove a frown;*
*It casts a magic spell, and brings depression to an end,*
*When wearing a stranger oftentimes becomes a friend.*
*The lonely love to see it and decide to wear it, too,*
*For they feel so much better when they look the same as you.*
*So what always is in fashion, something special all can wear?*
*It's a smile that's so uplifting, showing someone that you care.*

– Chrissy Greenslade.

## Sunday — March 4

WHAT do ordinary people have in common with saints? Anything at all?

They say every saint has a past, meaning they weren't always the people they ended up being.

And even while doing the things that made their reputation as pious men and women, most of them would have struggled with their own doubts and shortcomings.

So, what kept them going? Well, Corrie ten Boom, the great advocate of forgiveness after World War II, often pointed to this verse by an unknown poet.

"Cowardly, wayward and weak, I change with the changing sky.
Today so eager and strong, tomorrow not caring to try.
But He never gives in, and we two shall win,
Jesus and I."

The thing that we all have in common with the saints is that, whether we are strong or weak, whether our lives are ordinary or extraordinary, we don't live them alone.

And with His help we will win through.

## Monday — March 5

WHAT makes one pianist different from another, or one violin player better than the previous one, or one trumpet player a legend while the others remain unknown?

Pablo Casals, the world-renowned cellist and conductor, once wrote on a score by way of an autograph for another musician, "Don't play the notes. Play the meaning of the notes."

Any musician can play notes. What's makes one player stand out from the rest is how he interprets those notes, what he understands them to mean, and the lifetime of experience (not all musical) he brings to that understanding.

If you imagine your life as an instrument then Senor Casals's advice still holds true.

Don't play it like everyone else does. Bring your own understanding to the experience, and live a unique symphony.

## Tuesday — March 6

I HAD to smile at the café menu a friend sent me from Australia. Part of it read, "Coffee" – $5. "A coffee, please" – $4. "Good morning. How are you? Could I have a coffee, please?" – $2.50.

Now, polite people don't do it to get a good deal on their morning coffee, but it does go a long way to smoothing out the day. Good manners, one way or another, get you more for less.

## Wednesday — March 7

ABRAHAM LINCOLN gave some good advice on facing up to life's troubles.

He said, "Be sure you put your feet in the right place, then stand firm."

But first of all, you'll notice, he said to stand in the right place. It's a fine thing to have principles and beliefs, but let us take a moment to make sure they are good ones.

## Thursday — March 8

THERE'S a demonstration trick favoured by boxers and martial artists. They line up six or eight candles over a distance of about six feet. Then, after a little showmanship, they jab a punch in the direction of the candles. The air-wave caused, if it's done right, blows out all the candles.

You might guess that this isn't going to be about boxing tips. Instead, I think, it's a perfect example of how our words and actions have consequences beyond themselves. The things we say and do will send "waves" out into the world. Let's make sure they are the kind that light candles of hope rather than blowing them out.

## Friday — March 9

A COMMON excuse for not rising above the demands of the day and working for the good of the community is that it just isn't practical. So people back away from caring for society and revert to caring for themselves. Lady Nancy Astor, the first female Member of Parliament, might have argued with that definition of practicality.

"The most practical thing in the world," she said, "is common sense – and common humanity!"

## Saturday — March 10

JAMIE and Tammas in J.M. Barrie's "When A Man's Single" were reassuring each other of their ordinariness. The one insisted he was not even uncommonly ordinary, while the other agreed he was just "middlin' ord'nary."

It reminded me of the representative of a particular church denomination who said, "The Franciscans are mighty when it comes to good works and there are none so up on book-learning as the Jesuits, but when it comes to humility there's none of them a patch on us."

Humility is fine and generally a good thing – but let's not let it go to our heads!

## Sunday — March 11

ON this Mothering Sunday I would like to share these words about his own mother from the great writer D.H. Lawrence.

He wrote of Lydia Lawrence, who was a pupil-teacher and a lace-factory worker before becoming a wife and mother, "She was my first great love. She was a wonderful, rare woman – you do not know: as strong and steadfast, and as generous as the sun.

"She could be as swift as a white whiplash, as kind and gentle as the warm rain, and as steadfast as the irreducible earth beneath us."

Why did I share those words? Because Lawrence said, "You do not know." And, if you have, or have had, a good mother then I am sure you do know!

It is only one of the many wonders of a mother that they can share so many attributes but still be uniquely special to every child.

## Monday — March 12

*I FOUND a little bookshop,*
*New books to read, perhaps?*
*But when I stepped inside it*
*I found it full of maps!*
*Such strange, enticing places,*
*Such unfamiliar routes,*
*Some more direct than others.*
*But who would give two hoots?*

*For life is like a journey,*
*Why take it at a run?*
*It's how we make that journey*
*That turns it into fun.*
*We each must make our own map,*
*Quite different and unique,*
*May yours enrich and lead you*
*To what you truly seek.*

*– Maggie Ingall.*

## Tuesday — March 13

A MAGICIAN gathered all his spells into three volumes and offered to sell them to a king. The king said the price was ridiculous, so the magician burned one book and offered the two remaining books for the same price.

The king refused. So, he burned one more and offered the last book – for the same price! The king, realising this was his last chance to own any spells, paid the full price.

When we are young and have plenty of days, friends or whatever, we might value them less. Perhaps we might take a lesson from the king and value each for what it is, rather than waiting until their main value becomes their rarity.

## Wednesday — March 14

CULTURES across the world can be hugely different. But does that mean the people are different? Well, let's take this old Chinese definition of happiness, for example – "Something to do, someone to love, and something to hope for."

Now, does that sound so foreign? It's a reminder, if it were needed, that once we get beyond the history and the politics, people are – happily – much the same the whole world over.

## Thursday — March 15

I STOOD at the sea-front, enjoying the kind of view that makes a heart soar. It seemed like I could see for ever. Then a wind-blown grain of sand hit my eye. Instant irritation led to a flood of tears. Seconds later, the majestic vista was gone, blocked from view by a tiny grain of sand and the resultant waterworks.

I turned my back and headed inland, frustrated that something so small could spoil something so grand.

Like a little fault, nurtured into a grudge, might block the whole of an otherwise wonderful person from a relationship.

Of course, the remedy is simple. Eyewash – and forgiveness!

Magical landscape.

*Siena, Italy*

HARRY and I were talking about the new fashion for "mindfulness". It's not new, of course, just an old practice rebranded. It's about living in the moment, not being held back by the past or living in fear of the future.

"I learned that in my hillwalking days," Harry told me. "If you focused on how high you had climbed you could spend the rest of the day admiring the view and getting nowhere.

"If you focused on how high the hill ahead of you was you might give up on the spot. But if you kept asking yourself, 'Can I take this step?' then you'd make it all the way to the summit."

My contribution wasn't as heroic as Harry's but it's a phrase worth remembering and it ties in with mindfulness pretty well.

"Yard by yard, life's awful hard. Inch by inch, you'll find it's a cinch."

## Saturday — March 17

*LISTEN to the silence*
*And feel it calm your mind,*
*Let the noisy world go by*
*As tangled thoughts unwind.*
*Learn the secret of the earth,*
*For nature works in peace,*
*And all things grow in silence*
*Their wonder to increase.*
*Take a little time for you*
*And let that peace begin,*
*Close your eyes, relax, be still,*
*And find it deep within.*
*So short a time, a precious time,*
*Serenity your goal,*
*Just listen to the silence*
*And let it soothe your soul.*

– Iris Hesselden.

## Sunday — March 18

AGED sixteen, long before he became an internationally acclaimed novelist, Leo Tolstoy studied law. Why do I mention this?

Because later in life he wrote of a law that not only trumped but could replace all the others. "Love is the highest and only law of human life," he wrote. "In the depths of his soul every human being – as we see most clearly in children – feels and knows this."

Jesus made a similar point when he said, "Let the little children come to me, and do not hinder them, for the kingdom of heaven belongs to such as these."

## Monday — March 19

HAVE you ever heard it said – or perhaps said it yourself – that there is just so much wrong with the world that nothing we could do could make a difference?

Well, that's one way of looking at the situation.

I much prefer the approach Dorothea Dix took. She was a social reformer in the 19th century and she once described her motivation thus – "In a world where there is so much to be done, I felt strongly impressed that there must be something for me to do."

There was. And there is, for each of us.

## Tuesday — March 20

TALKING about hardships that had come into his life, Uncle Bert admitted that not all of the worries of the world had come his way. But he had received his fair share.

"They took from me the easy optimism I had in my youth," he told me. "They took from me people and things I loved. But they also left something behind."

I remember wondering what on earth it could have been. Then he gifted me a nugget of wisdom I have carried with me since.

"The unshakeable belief that no darkness is so great that we ourselves cannot light a match in it."

## Wednesday — March 21

THEODORE ROOSEVELT was president of the United States for seven years and is generally acknowledged as one of the greats. But, despite being busy with matters national and international, he also found time to draw up a list of the different types of birds he saw in Washington D.C. There were 93 species spotted during his years in office, with more than half of them actually making an appearance in the White House gardens.

Isn't it a comforting thought that, be it in farms, fields, towns and even the world's great centres of power, Nature carries on doing her beautiful thing regardless of what we may be up to?

Perhaps, like Roosevelt, we simply need to take time away from what we think is important to appreciate what's really important.

## Thursday — March 22

AELRED of Rievaulx was a 12th-century Northumbrian monk who made a big impact on the spiritual and political life of Britain. He was an advisor to King David of Scotland, Henry VII of England, and an emissary to the Pope.

And he identified a universal medicine!

"No medicine is more valuable, none more efficacious, none better suited to the cure of all our ills, than a friend to whom we may turn in time of trouble, and with whom we may share our happiness in time of joy."

## Friday — March 23

ON this day in 1743 King George II heard Handel's "Messiah" for the first time. He stood up during the Hallelujah Chorus, so everyone else had to, instigating a tradition that has continued to this day.

People suggested he stood to ease his gout, or that being slightly deaf, he mistook the tune for the National Anthem. But perhaps this most powerful of men simply felt the need to stand, respectfully, when praises were being offered to the greatest King?

**Up, up and away!**

*Cappadocia, Turkey.*

## Saturday — March 24

I ASKED my neighbour if I could bring her anything back from town.

"A pack of cheap pens, please," she said, "but not blue. I don't like blue. And, anyway, blue doesn't suit what I want to do."

So, I came back with a pack of pens. Blue pens! I hadn't done it on purpose. The best excuse I could come up with was that she had said "blue" so often it just stuck in my mind.

Words have that power. So, let's make sure the words we use most often – which will leave an impression – leave a positive impression and they don't leave anyone feeling blue.

## Sunday — March 25

VINCENT VAN GOGH wasn't one of the most stable of sources. He had down times and destructive days, but when he got it right he really got it right. Like his take on getting to know God.

"I always think that the best way to know God is to love many things. Love a friend, a wife, something, whatever you like. But love with a serious intimate sympathy, with strength, intelligence, and always try to know deeper, better, and more. That leads to God."

After all, we do say God is love. What better way to find him than by loving the best we can?

## Monday — March 26

THE Quaker poet and anti-slavery activist John Greenleaf Whittier had a particular idea of what heaven would be like. He wrote –

"The tissue of the life to be
We weave with colours all our own,
And in the field of Destiny
We reap as we have sown."

Of course, no-one knows what heaven will really be like. But if we thought we were planting seeds for Paradise, would it change the way we lived in this world?

And if there was room for improvement, oughtn't we to make it? For the sake of this world as much as for the next.

## Tuesday — March 27

WINTER had departed but spring didn't seem to have arrived yet. The Lady of the House and I ventured out.

The grass by the path, which had grown so tall the previous summer, was now straw-like and beaten flat by the wind and the rain.

"I imagine a lot of people feel like that," I said, feeling my age.

"And others are very glad of it," my sweetheart replied. She picked up a stick and lifted some of the grass. Beneath what I had seen as the detritus of winter lay green shoots – lots of them!

"Last year's grass might look beaten down," she explained, "but how else could it do the very important work of sheltering and protecting the generation to come? Those shoots wouldn't have survived on their own."

We walked on, me having learned a lesson from humble grass (and my sweetheart). If I must be old, then let it be for a purpose. And let that purpose be encouraging the future.

## Wednesday — March 28

BENJAMIN FRANKLIN was a statesman, an inventor, a publisher, a musician, a postmaster, a scientist, a civic activist, a Founding Father of the United States – he was a real over-achiever!

The key to getting so much done may have resided in a notion of his called the 13 Virtues. In an effort to be the very best person he could possibly be, Mr Franklin drew up a list of things he ought to aspire to. And he checked his progress on them every day.

They included moderation in eating and drinking, letting all aspects of his life have their place and time, not spending money unless it was to do good for himself or others, wronging no person, thinking innocently and justly, and imitating Jesus Christ in humility.

Did he succeed? Not always. His increasing girth in portraits show that moderation in food and drink was a struggle, for example. But did he benefit from trying? Undoubtedly!

If we set ourselves high standards we will, inevitably, fall short. But we will still rise higher in the attempt than if we had set no standards at all.

Afternoon tea.

## Thursday — March 29

**I** **DO** enjoy great words of wisdom. Usually they come from great figures of the past. But, sometimes, you find them in the mundane; in the here and now.

The man heading towards the shop door was putting his purchases into his bag. A woman who happened to be close by stepped over and opened the door for him. His face must have showed his surprise and I heard her say, "I'm here anyway. So I might as well be a help."

She was no great philosopher or religious leader. In truth, I don't even know her name. But can you imagine the difference it would make to the world if everyone adopted her words as their own philosophy?

"I'm here anyway. So I might as well help."

## Friday — March 30

**A** **SEEKER** once (supposedly) asked a wise man, "Which is greater, to love, or to be loved?"

The wise man replied, "Have you ever seen a bird fly with only one wing?"

Each of them is wonderful in its own right, but only to focus on one is like believing the only side the moon has is the one it presents to us, or like inhaling without exhaling.

If you want to know love, you need to know all of love. So, learn to give it. And learn to receive it.

## Saturday — March 31

**D** **ESPITE** English being my favourite subject at school, I never really learned about nouns, verbs, adverbs, pronouns, etc. I can make a guess at some of them, but they never really stuck in my mind. So, I am always happy to take the advice of an expert on them.

Bertha von Suttner won a Nobel Prize in 1905 and that qualifies her as an expert in my book. So, I am very happy to agree with her opinion of the two most beautiful verbs in the world.

What are they? "To love" and "to help."

# April

## Sunday — April 1

THE young man who bought the cottage at the edge of town has been there for half a year, but he's a busy man and we have only ever exchanged polite hellos.

On our morning stroll around town the Lady of the House had admired his new lawn. It seemed a little bland to me but I nobly refrained from comment. Then I noticed he hadn't actually cut his grass recently and he slipped a little further down in my estimation.

A few walks later we saw the leaves and then the lawn was patterned by bright and beautiful tulips. It seems he had laid in bulbs before he laid the turf.

"Well," my sweetheart said in an approving tone, "it just goes to show. Doesn't it?"

I nodded sagely for a few seconds before giving up the pretence.

"What? What does it show?"

"Simply that you never know what's beneath the surface," she squeezed my hand, "of grass or of new neighbours."

## Monday — April 2

I ALWAYS tried to do the right thing," Jim told me. "Even if it meant ignoring the little voice that kept asking, 'What's in it for me?'"

His daughter Anna is eighteen. She recently told her dad that everywhere she goes she meets someone who knows him. And it's always a positive experience. I can testify that Jim isn't famous or conventionally influential, he is just known as a good, honest man. It's almost like his reputation – built on all those times he chose to do the right thing – has become firm ground his daughter can stand on, or an umbrella under which she can shelter.

"So now, at last, I know what was in it for me," Jim told me.

A good reputation; more important – and useful – than we might expect!

## Tuesday — April 3

PEOPLE often bemoan the state of the world these days, suggesting there was a wonderful time (usually when they were children) when the world was a better place. Someone recently asked if I thought the world was a worse place these days. In reply I asked, "Worse than during World War II? Worse than during World War I?"

On a lighter note I laughed at the super-confident Peanuts character Lucy who asked, "How could the world be getting worse with me in it? Ever since I was born the world has shown a distinct improvement!"

Now, we don't have to be as conceited as Lucy, but the fact remains that we have a say in how good, bad or indifferent the world is today, tomorrow and the next day. So what's the world going to be like with you in it?

## Wednesday — April 4

THE preacher Charles Spurgeon might easily have been compared to a lighthouse. His faith shone out and many saw it. But not everyone is called to that role, and he acknowledged that when he said, "If you cannot be a lighthouse, you can at least be a night-light."

A little light in someone's darkness might be more important than a mighty beam shining across the sea.

## Thursday — April 5

A FINAL rinse, and raindrops fall,
The washing's nearly done,
The freshness so welcoming with fragrance, lightly spun.
Our world is washed anew today and all pegged out to dry,
The bright green leaves are spotless
As the breezes softly sigh.
On lea and lane and window-pane in every tuck and fold
Spick and span is nature, a pleasure to behold.
                                        – Dorothy McGregor.

## Friday — April 6

JONATHAN enjoys playing golf as often as he can. But he's not very good at it, so he doesn't waste money on big-name golf balls, reasoning that he is only likely to have them for a short while anyway.

Despite that, he has a bag full of top-of-the-range golf balls which he found while searching for his own.

"It works out well for me," he said with a laugh. "But I have to be out there, and I have to lose a lot of balls to find these new ones."

Being "out there" and involved in whatever your challenge may be is half the battle. The rewards for your efforts will surprise you and, gradually, you'll find yourself spending less time in life's rough and more on the green.

## Saturday — April 7

I DON'T remember the name of the church. I'm not even sure of the city or what I was doing there. But it was an unexpected find – a small traditional church that a bustling city-centre had grown up around. Its doors were open and a sign invited passers-by to come in and sit a while.

So I did.

It was many years ago and I remember nothing else about it. But I remember the gift of peace amidst the bustle. And I carry it with me even today.

## Sunday — April 8

ONE of the wonders of the 20th century was that apartheid South Africa transitioned to democracy without war breaking out. Bishop Desmond Tutu put that down to the power of prayer.

"We have been prayed for, you know," he said. "This is a miracle. It is not our doing. We've been on the intercessions list of the world for a long time. And it works. Yeah, man, it works!"

If God could do that through prayer, what conflict in your life could He not resolve?

## Monday — April 9

IS there anything that can't be made artistic or poetic? I only ask because of the gutter covers in the pedestrian areas of Perth town centre.

They have been designed to imitate Edvard Munch's painting, the Scream. I wonder if the designer had in mind how the rain-water must feel as it tumbles from the street into the darkness below.

It's a challenge to each of us, nonetheless. If drains can be made beautiful, then what aspect of our lives can't?

## Tuesday — April 10

IT was a joke about a man who wanted the cheapest hearing aid possible. The salesman gave him an ear-piece attached to a string, advising him to tuck the end of the string into his pocket.

"Of course, it doesn't work," he explained, "but when people see it they will talk louder."

Actually, other people are often only too happy to accommodate our difficulties and worries. They're a nice bunch, in the main. What we have to do is find our equivalent of that piece of string – our way of letting them know what it is we need.

## Wednesday — April 11

THE Cave of Melody, also known as Fingal's Cave, on the island of Staffa has inspired more than just melody. Mendelssohn wrote "The Hebrides Overture" after visiting it, Jules Verne wrote about it in a novel, J.M.W. Turner immortalised it in paint, James Macpherson named it Fingal's Cave in his poems.

But it was formed in fire and tectonic upheaval. The basalt pillars were shaped by unimaginable temperatures. The caves themselves were shaped by bubbling gasses.

Tough times indeed! But, in the end, a place that inspired peace, creativity and beauty in others.

Something to remember the next time we find ourselves under pressure.

## Thursday — April 12

A COMPANY of architects specialised in care homes and had a policy of sending their trainees to live in similar homes. They didn't just live there, they had ear-plugs to simulate degrees of deafness, spectacles with the wrong lenses, fingers taped together to create a loss of dexterity, weights on their ankles, and so on.

They were walking in the shoes of the people whose homes they would be designing.

Did it make them better architects? I can't say. But the boss of the company said they came back with hearts 10 times as big as they went away with.

## Friday — April 13

HAVE you ever heard anyone say, "What have I got to be thankful for?" I have. Too many times.

Rather than point out the things they should actually be grateful for, we might explain (if they would listen) that gratitude itself is something to be thankful for.

As the poet John Milton explained, "Gratitude bestows reverence, allowing us to encounter everyday epiphanies, those transcendent moments of awe that change for ever how we experience life and the world."

I am very thankful for gratitude!

## Saturday — April 14

LITTLE children might look in awe at a bouquet of hot-house flowers – but they would play with daisies, buttercups and dandelions.

I wonder if Thérèse of Lisieux had children (or others in a humble position in life) in mind when she wrote, "The splendour of the rose and the whiteness of the lily do not rob the little violet of its scent nor the daisy of its simple charm. If every flower wanted to be a rose, spring would lose its loveliness."

## Sunday — April 15

THE pastor had set up four prayer stations around the church; one a table with bread on it for giving thanks, another with a notepad and bin for writing down and discarding confessions, yet another where candles might be lit, and the last a quiet corner to simply be in the presence of God.

Being no-nonsense men, my neighbour and I did not participate, both of us sitting with our arms folded. But in the spirit of the thing I leaned sideways and asked, "Is there something you would pray about?"

He thought for a moment, smiled, and said, "He will work it out."

Those of us who pray might do it in any number of ways, but we would all benefit from such simple assurance that they will be answered.

## Monday — April 16

THE packing room of the food-bank was hot and poorly ventilated. The volunteers were working hard but niggles were beginning to show, tempers were getting a little frayed.

I took a walk to the door where I met a woman who was unhappily (I thought) examining the bags of food she had been given.

"Not enough?" I asked.

"Too much, if anything," she replied.

She told me of a life turned upside down, of the children depending on her, how she hadn't wanted to come along, but how glad she was that she had. Her most immediate concern now was how she could she ever thank us.

I assured her that every tin and packet was gladly given by people who cared and the best she could do for them was to help someone else when she was in a position to do so.

We said goodbye and I returned to the packing room and told the story. People nodded, nobody said much, we went back to work. But the atmosphere was lighter, I could see more smiles – and someone started singing.

**Golden daffodils.**

Craigievar Castle, Scotland.

## Tuesday — April 17

I KNOW pastors who prepare their sermons in the hope that one person is powerfully touched by them. They understand that they don't need to know who that person is. An author friend has his free copies of his books sent to a care home for teenagers in the hope they might be encouraged to read and learn. He has never met any of them. But he keeps them in mind when he is writing.

Those of us who don't preach or write can still make a difference in the lives of others through the words we speak. And because we never know who will be affected by them – or when – we should try our best to make those words good ones.

## Wednesday — April 18

I DO enjoy discovering words the English language has no direct translation for. Like the Portuguese word *saudade*.

Apparently, it describes the emptiness left inside you when you are missing someone. But there's more! It's that specific kind of emptiness that can only be filled by beautiful memories.

A sad word, perhaps, but isn't it a wonderfully positive notion that most of our longings are created because of beautiful memories? So what else is better equipped to soothe our *saudade*?

Memories. While the rest of the world moves on they remain one of life's most precious gifts.

## Thursday — April 19

THE church of St Mary's on the Berkshire Downs is worth a visit in its own right. But it has the added attraction of the "Aldworth Giants," statues of the lords and ladies of the de la Beche family placed there in the 1340s.

On your way to visit some of man's artistic and architectural masterworks you might walk past the tree outside the church without a second glance. But it is a yew tree that has lived and grown on that same spot since some time in the 12th century. God's quite the artist himself!

## Friday — April 20

*SEEK a fresh goal every day,*
*Look on all things new,*
*Show a smile along the way,*
*Let happiness shine through.*
*Don't give up, if plans may fail,*
*Make another start;*
*Keep a trust if hope is frail,*
*Find faith within your heart.*
*Set aside a time to care*
*And then you'll find it's true,*
*A kindness passed around to share*
*Will be returned to you!*

– Elizabeth Gozney.

## Saturday — April 21

THE following is advice printed in a magazine in 1934 on how to relate to "the other fellow."

"Always believe the best about him – until you know the worst. Even then, question if you actually know it. Make certain you are not believing rumour, or simply misunderstanding him. Be cautious. Be charitable. Look for the best in him.

"And if he turns out simply to be a bad lot, why, your work isn't finished then. Offer him your hand and, by your fine example, set about trying to make him a better lot."

Old-fashioned? Perhaps. Still useful? I'd say so.

## Sunday — April 22

I HAD an apology to make. My first instinct was to make it later, but a wiser voice said, "Do it now." So, I did. As it happened, I wouldn't have got the chance later.

As some unknown soul said, "You don't keep grace in the freezer for later. It's an endlessly available gift, but its use-by date is always now."

## Monday — April 23

MOLLY works as a volunteer in an animal sanctuary. The other day a well-to-do-looking woman came in looking for a dog. It was to replace a much-loved family pet, she explained. She seemed particularly keen on a scraggy-looking mutt Molly had always thought had a particular sparkle in its eye.

Molly explained the dog had been a stray and in quite a bad way when it was brought to them. Then she said that the sanctuary would have to run certain checks to make sure the dog was going to a good home.

"Oh, it's not for me," the woman explained. "But I know it'll be well taken care of. You see, it's for a couple who took me in fifteen years ago when I was a stray and I was in a bad way."

Molly tells me the checks will still be done, but with a reference like that she doubts there'll be a problem.

## Tuesday — April 24

HARRY has been working hard on his family tree. He has names on it going back to the 1800s.

But it has often upset him to think that all he has of these family members are bare facts – addresses and dates of birth and death. After all, these were the people without whom he wouldn't be here!

Then, through the kindness of a recently discovered relative, Harry got to read a very old letter. Some of it concerned his great-great-grandad. It read:

"I wish I had time to tell you about John. Foreman, bookbinder, and amateur botanist. Kind, wise, paunchy, jocular, devoted to whist drives and evenings out with his brother-in-law. I see him yet wiping his walrus moustache this way and that, over some yarn."

Now John could have left behind money or family heirlooms. He didn't.

Instead he left behind the memory of a happy and well-loved family man and, as far as Harry's concerned, that's what real treasure looks like.

## Wednesday — April 25

DO you ever write a "To-do" list?
 Mine are generally full of mundane things like "Buy milk" or "Fix the fence". As might be expected, the country superstar Johnny Cash has much more interesting to-do lists, although they weren't as exotic as might be expected. A man of strong passions, he had to fight for the good in his life and fight against the bad.

This was reflected in one list that said:
1.   Don't smoke
2.   Kiss June (his wife)
3.   Don't kiss anyone else!

Remembering the milk is all very important, but along with the grocery list we could do worse than keep a list of the things we need to do and not do for the kind of life we want to have.

## Thursday — April 26

OH, you always see the bright side," someone said to me. And it's true. The conversation left me wondering what my friend saw.

It reminded me of an experiment. A psychologist showed students a thirty-second film of two teams playing basketball. They asked the students to count how many times the team in white passed the ball.

Then they ran the film again, pointing to the man in a gorilla suit walking across the court. None of the students had noticed him before. They were so intent on what they were looking for.

Given that it seems to be a choice, I have to wonder . . . why doesn't everyone see the bright side?

## Friday — April 27

THE Persian poet Kahlil Gibran wrote, "Wake at dawn with a winged heart and be thankful for another day of loving."

Of course, whether you spend that day loving will be entirely up to you, but the decision you make regarding that will play a big part in deciding whether or not your heart soars when you wake up.

## Saturday — April 28

IF the sky hadn't been grey, if the sun hadn't been obscured, if the field hadn't been ploughed and beaten down again by the rain, then the coloured twine the farmer used to tie the gate up wouldn't have seemed so vividly luminescent.

George spotted the contrast of the bright colour against the drab scene. He photographed it, entered the photo in a competition, and won a prize.

If a dreich day can make some old twine stand out to such good effect, then think on other hard times and how they might be the perfect setting for us to shine in.

## Sunday — April 29

IT would be wonderful if good times would come and never leave. Instead, they are constantly being renewed. That process of renewal, unfortunately, leaves gaps for less than happy times to fill.

The 17th-century English poet Anne Bradstreet recognised this. But she also recognised a solution. She wrote –
"I have a shelter from the storm
A shadow from the fainting heat:
I have access unto your throne
You who are God so wondrous great."

Perhaps if good times did last for ever we might forget that the best times will be around that throne – where there is room for everyone!

## Monday — April 30

THE composer Handel had his fair share of ups and downs. While he was struggling to make a name for himself he often chose to play "quality" music instead of whatever was popular at the time.

When told that his insistence would result in him playing to empty theatres he supposedly replied, "Ah, but think of the acoustics!"

Handel eventually proved his detractors wrong, but it takes a strong personality to stick by the things that mean the most to you in times when others would take the easier, more popular, option.

# May

## Tuesday — May 1

*OF all the flowers fit for posies,*
*None are as fair as Briar Roses,*
*Their heady perfume fills the breeze*
*That stirs the leaves of willow trees.*
*They tumble over dry stone walls,*
*With wild abandon that enthralls,*
*They charm us till the evening closes,*
*The petals of the Briar Roses.*

– Brian H. Gent.

## Wednesday — May 2

IF you get the chance to walk the road up and over the island of Big Cumbrae, do take it! Not only will you be rewarded by excellent views of Arran, Kintyre and the islands to the north, but you will, at the highest point, find the Glaid Stone.

I imagine this rocky outcrop got its name from countless walkers reaching the end of their climb and saying, "I'm glaid that's a' over!"

There, you will find a plaque with a Bible verse I once misread. It says, *Oh, Lord, how manifold are thy works! In wisdom hast Thou made them all: the earth is full of Thy riches.* Except, I read it as *the earth is full of Thy niches.* And I started thinking of all the normally unobserved corners we stumble on where we find unexpected peace and beauty.

The Lady of the House (gently, of course) put me right when I started waxing lyrical on my mistaken theme.

Ah, but was I mistaken? Yes! But that doesn't take away from the fact that the glory of Creation is expressed both in panoramic vista like those available from the Glaid Stone and in the hidden niches it is our delight to find by accident.

Manifold are His works, indeed!

## Thursday — May 3

THE chimes of Big Ben in London aren't the same as the "bongs." The tune of the chimes comes from the aria, "I Know My Redeemer Liveth" and words from it (from the Book of Job) are on a plaque in the clock room. It reads, *Lord, through this hour, be Thou our guide; so by Thy power no foot shall slide.*

The dependability of Big Ben is important. The bongs are broadcast live around the world and a lot of effort is put into keeping them as accurate as possible.

There are things in this world, however, more dependable than Big Ben. In this world, and beyond it, we can depend on the One the words were written in praise of.

## Friday — May 4

BEN lives near the coast and has a beautiful collection of sea-glass, some of which he gives to his daughter Pam who makes jewellery.

"Sea glass," he told me, "starts off as bottles, or glass floats. It's either broken when it goes into the sea or it's broken by the rocks. Then the fragments are tossed about, scraped against the sea-bed, and gradually worn smooth to the point where they acquire a new and rather beautiful appearance."

The next time you feel like life is spinning you around, pulling you this way and that, think of the journey of the sea glass and remember, you might come out more beautiful than you went in.

## Saturday — May 5

THROUGHOUT World War II "The Times" printed a series of quotes under the title "Old And True". The hope was that ancient wisdom would help raise national morale.

These days are not as tumultuous as those, but they have their troubles, and we could do worse than follow the examples of "The Times" and someone else whose wisdom is old and true.

To paraphrase St Paul, whatever is noble, right, pure, lovely, admirable; in difficult times, think about such things.

**Mirror image.**

*Loch Ard, Scotland*

## Sunday — May 6

ST ENODOC'S church in Cornwall was almost buried under drifting sand. Restorations began in 1912 and now it is a curiously beautiful place to visit. But the unusual thing about the 12th-century church is that it seems to have served no known community.

Perhaps it once did and the clues to the community now lie under the sand. Or perhaps it was placed on top of an older worship site to assert the presence of the church.

But for those with a more romantic inclination a church in the middle of nowhere, for no discernible purpose, is a good reminder that every part of this Creation is worth praise and giving thanks for.

## Monday — May 7

DAVID and Julie were admiring the generosity of a friend who gave his coat to a man who was living on the streets. Then Julie turned to David saying, "You do things like that. Remember that time you gave your holiday pay to your workmate who needed to get her children to a new, safe, house and didn't have the rent?"

David didn't remember – but Julie assured me that's what he had done.

Elizabeth Bibesco, the English poet, described that perfectly when she wrote, "Blessed are those who can give without remembering and take without forgetting."

## Tuesday — May 8

IT was a wilderness garden, or simply neglected. At some point someone had dumped some aluminium fencing sections there and the garden had grown around it.

But among and around the fencing (and nowhere else) grew scarlet flowers.

It was almost as if nature had said to the ore that had been taken from the ground – broken down, heated, mixed, remade, used and then abandoned – "Here. Rest. And I'll make you pretty for a while."

WHEN, back in the 1820s, the clergyman and essayist Sydney Smith heard that his friend Lady Georgiana Morpeth was suffering from low spirits, he sent her a list of remedies.

•Live as well as you dare

•Read amusing books, watch entertaining plays

•Do good and endeavour to please many of all stations

•Make the room where you commonly sit gay and pleasant

•Don't underrate yourself, but do yourself justice

•Make no secret of your low spirits to your friends

•Keep good blazing fires

•And attend to the effects a good cup of tea might have on you

Much has changed since those days, but the human condition is still as it was, and Reverend Smith's remedies would surely still raise anyone's spirits, whether they were low to start off with or not.

## Thursday — May 10

*FOR ever the ocean will sing to the shore*
*And whisper of far-away lands,*
*Its songs will find echoes in hearts and in minds*
*As it smooths and caresses the sands.*
*But now is the time and the moment is yours*
*To set all your thoughts flying free,*
*So join with the wind and the birds in the air*
*It's time now to sing to the sea.*
*So walk on the sea-shore and drink in the air*
*And smell the wet seaweed and shells,*
*The ozone will lift you in body and soul,*
*The waves will release magic spells.*
*The work-a-day world will fade out of sight*
*And any dark shadows will flee,*
*Be closer to nature and lift up your voice*
*It's time now to sing to the sea!*

– Iris Hesselden.

## Friday — May 11

**D**ECADES after her time as a Hollywood icon, Audrey Hepburn is still regarded as one of the most beautiful and elegant women ever. Part of the attraction, I believe, lay in her understanding of beauty.

"The beauty of a woman," she wrote, "is not in the clothes she wears, the figure she carries, or the way she combs her hair. The beauty of a woman must be seen in her eyes, because that is the doorway to her heart, the place where love resides."

And, gentlemen, you may not be Hollywood starlets – but the same applies to you!

## Saturday — May 12

**W**E all go through times of emotional or spiritual darkness. When it happens, accept that it was always going to happen – but don't consent to stay in it. Go slowly, taking care, like you would in any dark place. Accept an outstretched hand if you find one. Develop the senses you don't use in the light and understand you have been prepared for this. And remember that darkness is nothing more than the preparation for growth for every seed that grows in the ground. Ready. Get Set. Grow!

## Sunday — May 13

**J**EREMY TAYLOR was chaplain to King Charles the First, Bishop of Down and Connor, and is often regarded as one of England's finest writers. Many of his thoughts are still worth sharing today, but I particularly like his take on love and friendship.

"The more we love," he wrote, "the better we are, and the greater our friendships are, the closer we are to God."

Nice thoughts – but with a hint that we have a role to play in it all. Love and friendship are "doing" words. Let's do them both to the best of our ability, and we will inevitably find ourselves closer to God.

Colours of nature.

St Ives harbour, Cornwall.

## Monday — May 14

OH, she looks for me," the checkout operator explained. "She needs things to be laid out just so. Some of the others don't understand. But I know how she likes things done. And I smile at her though she never smiles back. So, she looks for me."

It's one thing to be kind and patient. It's another more wonderful thing to be the person people look for because they need someone to be kind and patient with them, and they know you will be.

## Tuesday — May 15

SHE would go on to become an internationally recognised writer, but when she was twenty years old Sylvia Plath had college and romance on her mind.

Preparing to return to college after the summer holidays, she wrote her "School Commandments." In them she reminded herself to keep up a cheerful front. This despite the fact that she was struggling with some of her work and the boy she liked was showing a certain amount of disdain.

She listed the essays she needed to write, the lecturers she could ask for help, and advised herself to keep cheerful – even when things were as bad as they could get.

Then, in a PS she added, "Remember – you are still a lot better off than 9/10ths of the world. Love, Syl!"

It's something I am sure most of us could truthfully say. And something worth remembering when we feel inclined to complain.

## Wednesday — May 16

SOME people talk the talk but don't always walk the walk. If we have beliefs people should know them without us having to tell them. They should know by how we live our lives.

As Jane Addams, the social reformer and Nobel Prize winner, said, "Action is indeed the sole medium of expression for ethics."

So, if you believe it . . . live it!

## Thursday — May 17

JUST up from the shore in Lamlash Bay sits a picture-postcard row of cottages. They look across the water to Holy Isle, and if you lived there you might be tempted to call your cottage something like "Sea View", "Island View" or "Bay View."

Being a nosy sort of chap, I always like to look behind the façade, so I took a walk along the path behind the cottages. Someone, with a view to getting their money's worth from the wonderful location, has built a row of box-like houses, perhaps as holiday homes.

Only seconds from the beach, their view consists entirely of the back of the cottages, their brick walls and outhouses – and their wheelie bins!

One of the owners obviously considered this when he had the name-plate made for his house, which he called Bucket View.

I hope he didn't mind me stopping for a double-take and then laughing. It reminded me that there is no situation that can't be made better by a good sense of humour.

## Friday — May 18

THE legend of the Gordian Knot has been around since before Alexander the Great, and it still keeps popping up. That's probably because so many people seem to find themselves facing problems in their lives that, apparently, have no solution.

Relationships, in particular, have always thrown up such knotty problems. And they often bring those relationships to an end when it seems that nothing further can be done. But there is always something that can be done.

When Alexander saw this fabled knot that no man could loosen he drew his sword and cut it in half.

If there is an unsolvable problem in your life, don't let that stop you from placing love before it, beside it and beyond it.

The problem may simply have to be left there (until it eventually disappears of its own accord), but the relationship, and the love, will go on.

## Saturday — May 19

LOUISE was recording a message on her local radio station for her disability group. She read the script flawlessly until she tripped over the phrase "insurmountable obstacles." Having got it wrong once, she fluffed it again and again . . . Until the recording engineer told her, "Just say "impossible problems" and I'll edit it in." So, she did.

The moral of the story being that a lot of insurmountable obstacles can actually be overcome, with a willing heart, some imagination, and a little skilful editing!

## Sunday — May 20

A COMMON greeting in both Austria and Germany is "Gruss Got." When we take our leave of someone in this country we tend to say "goodbye."

"Gruss Got" means "God greets you" or "I greet you in God's name." "Goodbye" is a contraction of the words, "God be with you."

They remind me of the verse from Deuteronomy: "You will be blessed when you come in and blessed when you go out."

In your coming and your going – be always with God.

## Monday — May 21

IT was a threatening misty morning." "The wind was furious." "All was cheerless and gloomy so we faced the storm." "The wind seized our breath."

So wrote Dorothy Wordsworth in her Grasmere Journals. Her account was actually more positive than these extracts suggest. They are simply indications of the day she and her party ploughed through to get to the point where her brother William was inspired to write the immortal line, "When all at once I saw a crowd; a host of golden daffodils."

The greatest beauties in this world don't often simply appear on our doorsteps. Sometimes, we must venture out and win them, and the venturing out itself is often a large part of the beauty we find.

Under blue skies.

*Northern Lights, Iceland.*

## Tuesday — May 22

*THERE runs a little grassy path that winds behind my home,*
*It passes by my garden gate, and always bids me roam.*
*For daisies, like a million stars, are scattered on its way.*
*It almost seems they call to me, "Come out, come out and play!"*
*And so I follow on and up, towards the windy hill*
*Where all the world is far away, and troubles further still.*
*It leads me through the woods and fields, beside the chalky stream*
*Where here in dappled shade I sit, to pause awhile and dream.*
*Until at last, with heart refreshed, I see the day grows late.*
*And once more, by the daisy path. I reach my own back gate.*

– Maggie Ingall.

## Wednesday — May 23

THE Lady of the House was explaining the term "a capella" to me. I had thought it described an unaccompanied vocal group, but it means to sing as you would in church, and it comes from the days when musical instruments weren't included so the voices had to try all the harder to reach Heaven on their own.

"So, they had to really mean it," I suggested. "Put their heart and soul into it."

"Perhaps," she said, smiling prettily. "Of course they might do even better to sing like you do when you really mean it." I had just enough time to smile proudly at being such a good example before she added, "Not like you do in church but like you do in the shower."

I didn't bother defending myself. I was already in enough of a lather.

## Thursday — May 24

THERE'S a lot to be said for the philosophy of walking a mile in someone else's shoes to better understand them. But I also like the notion of accepting that their shoes will be an uncomfortable fit for you, as yours would be for them, and simply walking a mile together, talking with each other.

74

## Friday — May 25

HAVE you ever seen one of those Where's Waldo, or Where's Wally, books? The point of them is to find the one distinctly dressed character on the page. That ought to be easy enough, but to make it more challenging the illustrator crams the page full of other objects, animals and characters. Every centimetre of each big page is filled with something interesting or exciting.

But, of course, finding those things isn't the point of the game, it is to find Wally (or Waldo). All those other drawings are nothing more than interesting distractions.

Finding what matters in this life can be a bit like searching for the main character in one of those books. The truth, or the purpose of it all, is there but life is crammed full of distractions.

Perhaps, if we are serious about finding the truth, we might borrow this prayer from the Danish theologian Soren Kierkegaard – "Lord, give us weak eyes for things which are of no account, and clear eyes for all your Truth."

And, like everything else, the more you practice the better at it you become; the more you look for the truth, the more you will find it.

## Saturday — May 26

WATCH out for the rainbow, its beauty behold,
Each delicate colour of pastels unfold.
A spectrum of nature to dazzle the eye
Though somehow uplifting, we cannot tell why!
Perhaps it's the feeling that comfort is found
In the wonder of nature we see all around
To give us at least a small breathing space
Apart from the everyday problems we face.
Perhaps in the colours the rainbow imparts
We may find inspiration to brighten our hearts;
For it's moments like these that bring grace to each day,
So watch for the rainbow – it's heading your way!

– Elizabeth Gozney.

## Sunday — May 27

THE praise band was rehearsing for a sermon on graceful giving. Frances, the singer, told me the discussion turned to those in the church who looked for a need and filled it.

"It seemed that people would do that for a while," she told me, "then they would get disillusioned. As if they expected something in return and didn't find it."

"So, does no-one in your church give gracefully – and keep doing it?" I asked. "Does no-one give for the sake of giving?"

"Yup!" she said, smiling widely. "Maybe only two or three, when I came to think of it. But they were the reason I sang that day."

Graceful giving. It's well worth singing about.

## Monday — May 28

THE sign by the motorway advertised land for sale. Seeing it reminded me of the words of the Dutch evangelist Corrie ten Boom. "If you are unhappy with your lot in life," she said, "build a service station on it!"

And make it one of the ones people look forward to visiting.

## Tuesday — May 29

JOE is a farmer. There are a fair number of dry-stane dykes on his farm and from time to time they need to be repaired. It's specialised work but Joe's dad passed on some useful tips.

"He showed me how to deal with it one space at a time. To find the stone that fit the best, to make sure that stone was a good 'un, fit it solidly . . . and then look at the next space."

As a result, Joe's repairs look to stand as long as the original wall.

Doing the best you can in the here-and-now, leaving the past behind (except what you learned from it) and not being distracted by the future (except what good sense suggests you prepare for), giving all your attention to the job in hand – that's how you build solid, dependable walls and solid, dependable lives.

## Wednesday — May 30

**HAVE** to be honest. I have never performed in front of thousands of people – except in my dreams! But I do know that the last thing performers see before they take to the stage in the Hydro in Glasgow is a neon sign encouraging them to "Gie it laldy!"

To give it laldy in Scots means to do whatever it is with pride in what you're doing, with as much enthusiasm as you can muster, and with all the energy you possess.

Now, most of us will never walk through that door, but each of us will tread the stage of our life daily.

Whether no-one turns up for the show or we have an enthusiastic audience, remember, your life is your performance. And you are the star of the show.

So, in whatever way works best for you . . . gie it laldy!

## Thursday — May 31

**ADMIT** I have never woven anything and wouldn't begin to know how to approach a loom. But for those who have mastered the craft it seems to be a very contemplative pastime, inspiring several philosophical notions. Like –

the idea that threads broken at the back of the tapestry will be held in place by the strong threads and still colour their part of the front of the picture.

the thought that it is enough for the weaver of faith to do their best work and trust the Lord will supply the thread.

the notion that a tapestry might seem chaotic on the back side and present a beautiful picture on the front side.

And these verses from "The Loom Of Time" by an anonymous poet –

"Not 'til the loom is silent and the shuttles cease to fly

Shall God reveal the pattern and reveal the reason why.

The dark threads were as needful in the weaver's skilful hand

As threads of gold and silver for the pattern which he planned."

# June

HARVARD UNIVERSITY'S longest-running research programme has been going for over three-quarters of a century, and it is still going. The Harvard Study of Adult Development asked to follow 724 boys, some poor and some well-to-do, asking questions about many different aspects of their lives.

Lots of things have been learned, but one result was the secret of happiness! It's not money, nor success, nor fame. After studying all those men (and their wives) for all those years, they came to the conclusion that secure, steady relationships were not only the key to happiness, they were also good for our health!

Want to be happy? Make good friends. Marry someone you can depend upon.

I don't know that we needed a decades-long study to tell us that – but isn't it nice to have it confirmed?

*DEAR Lord, you know I long for*
*A faith that's strong and sure,*
*That holds me when I'm anxious,*
*Or lost or insecure.*
*A faith which questions daily*
*Yet hankers not for proof,*
*A faith which seeks for answers*
*Yet knows its inner truth.*
*Dear Lord, I'm still imperfect,*
*My faith may sometimes fail,*
*I am not always trusting when fears and doubts assail,*
*Yet hold me, if you will, Lord, whene'er my faith feels small,*
*For this I know for certain –*
*Your love won't let me fall.*

– Maggie Ingall.

## Sunday — June 3

HE had searched for days and was about to give up when a Salvation Army officer suggested they pray, asking God to help him to find his missing friend. He was impatient, but she insisted.

The amens still echoed in the hostel hallway when a man walked in. He wasn't the missing friend – but he knew where he was! The searcher and his missing friend were reunited within half an hour.

A nice story? The truth. I was the searcher.

## Monday — June 4

THESE days we have embassies all over the world. But before that it was the duty of a king or a country to welcome and provide for the ambassadors any other king or country might send to them.

Peter Maurin, who wrote "Easy Essays On Peace And Justice" in 1934, had this interesting view of ambassadorship.

"The Greeks used to say that people in need were ambassadors of God. As God's ambassadors they should be given food, clothing and shelter by those able to give it."

As I mentioned earlier, we should expect to be treated in a similar fashion when we arrive at the court of the one who sent them.

## Tuesday — June 5

I LEANED on the fence watching a pastime I thought long gone and reliving my own adventures with jam-jar and net.

The farmer drove up and the tadpole hunters scrambled up from his stream and scattered.

"Perhaps," he said sternly to me, "they didn't see the *No Trespassing* sign you were leaning on!" As I prepared to explain, his face lit in a smile.

"The law says we have to put signs up. But I used to go tadpoling myself. And the best ones were always found where we weren't supposed to be!"

**Nature's beauty.**

*Cascade des Anglais waterfall, Corsica.*

## Wednesday — June 6

BEAUTIFUL thoughts are nice, but, really, they're just thoughts. Aren't they? John Ruskin, the 19th-century art critic and philanthropist, thought differently.

"What palaces we may build of beautiful thoughts," he wrote. "Treasure houses which care cannot disturb, nor pain make gloomy, nor poverty take away – houses built without hands for our souls to live in."

Now, who wouldn't want their own treasure house? Especially one that costs nothing to build. Think about it – but think beautifully!

## Thursday — June 7

OUR young neighbours are just back from a holiday they described as heaven on earth. Or, they thought so until they walked a little too far along the beach and discovered armed guards around the place to keep the locals away. That rather took the shine off.

When you do find heaven on earth you can walk as far as you like, because you will be carrying it with you. And you will be sharing it with whoever you meet.

## Friday — June 8

ANDREW JACKSON, the seventh President of the United States, was no-one's idea of a regular church-goer. He went so far as to build a church for his wife – but he never joined her there in worship.

Aged seventy, he asked the elders of that same church if he could join. They told him he would have to show forgiveness first. This was a problem for Jackson. He found the grudges he had held the longest were the most difficult to let go. But, eventually, he offered forgiveness to all who had hurt him.

During the first service he attended people were amazed to see tears rolling down the cheek of this old and powerful man. They could only guess they were tears of relief.

Forgiveness, no matter how long it takes, really is a gift you give to yourself.

## Saturday — June 9

I WATCHED Harry tend his plants and wondered (out loud) how they would cope without him.

"Well," he considered the question, "they'd get by without the fertiliser. I don't imagine they would miss the pruning. I water them regularly, of course, but they'd survive on the rain we get. The one thing they couldn't do without is sunshine. I can position them the best I can to receive it, but I can't supply it."

As he returned to his work my mind turned to love, which we can position ourselves and others to receive, and which we can reflect, but we don't supply it. And without it we would surely wither.

But, like the sunshine, it is provided.

## Sunday — June 10

JOHN HARVEY KELLOGG gave the world its most popular breakfast cereal – Corn Flakes. His distant relative Florence Scripps Kellogg gave the world a beautiful morning prayer which begins,

"Each morning when I wake, I say,
'I place my hand in God's today!'
I know he'll walk close by my side
My every wandering step to guide."

Perhaps, as we sit down to our breakfast each day, we might offer up a similar prayer.

## Monday — June 11

WHEN it comes to friends, we look for the person who is right for us. But may God save us from looking for the perfect person. The English poet Alexander Pope hit the nail squarely on the head when he wrote, "My friend is not perfect – neither am I – and so we suit each other admirably!"

Besides, if our friend was perfect, and we were perfect, where would be the room for forgiveness? And forgiveness is the strengthening ingredient in every relationship.

## Tuesday — June 12

IN 1924 the New York Symphony Orchestra played Beethoven's Symphony Number 9 to an audience in the Carnegie Hall. I am sure the musicians and the music lovers all enjoyed the experience.

The performance was broadcast live via radio. The broadcaster (and the people who built the radios) all did their job well and an audience of many more thousands enjoyed the concert.

For some time afterwards the conductor had messages of appreciation from people who had enjoyed listening to the piece. But the letter from Helen Keller, who had been deaf and blind almost from birth, must have been a great surprise.

A friend had unscrewed the cover from her radio. She had placed her hand on the speaker and enjoyed "an ocean of heavenly vibrations."

When we put good, or truth, or beauty into the world we never know who might benefit from it and it often does good in ways we could never imagine.

Sometimes we simply have to do our bit – and stand by to be amazed by the results.

## Wednesday — June 13

YOU wouldn't think there was anything remarkable about the little brown box Alice keeps with her family photos. It only holds two sheets of notepaper and an old pair of spectacles. The pencilled words on the paper, written over 60 years ago, are faded.

The box once belonged to Alice's gran. The letter was the only one her grandad ever wrote to his wife. He wrote it while he was abroad with the Forces and missing home and hearth.

Gran outlived Grandad by 23 years and every night before bed she would read his letter then tuck it, with her spectacles, into the little box which then went under her pillow. Now it's one of Alice's treasures.

Gentlemen! If you've never written your wife a love letter, if you think such things are just silly nonsense that don't mean anything, read this . . . and think on.

## Thursday — June 14

DOGS aren't built for going down stairs easily. Which is probably why a visit from a puppy made it into Great-aunt Louisa's diary.

"Having rapidly attained the landing," she wrote, "the darling little thing looked down on us from above and his nose sank to the boards in fear. No amount of encouragement from below enabled him to trust those little legs to the descent.

"Then Father's hound slipped past us and up to the puppy. The older dog ran downstairs and up again. Then it hunched down beside the pup and, muzzle by muzzle, they descended. Soon, the excited pup had to be banned from the bedrooms!

"And I was left thinking, 'That's fellowship. That's friendship. That's discipleship!'"

## Friday — June 15

THE novelist George Eliot believed the world was becoming a better place, despite the intentions of those in power. She wrote, "The growing good of the world is partly dependent on unhistoric acts. That kings are not so bad to you and me as they might be is half owing to the people who lived faithful hidden lives."

In other words, you don't have to make the pages of the history books to make a difference.

## Saturday — June 16

WHEN the French poet Charles Baudelaire wrote a "fan letter" to the German composer Richard Wagner, he ended with a rather unusual post script.

He wrote, "I do not set down my address because you might think I wanted something of you."

It would be sad if people could not take a compliment without suspicion, but it is a wonderful thing to offer praise, or help, knowing they need never feel compelled to return the favour.

A gift well received that can never be returned is, paradoxically enough, a gift already received by the giver.

God's glorious colours.

*Appalachian Mountains, North America.*

## Sunday — June 17

THE minister was telling the story of the Prodigal Son to a group of teenagers. He told how the son wasted his inheritance and found himself impoverished, worse off than the pigs he tended, before finally deciding to return home.

"And what do you think the moral of the story is?" he asked.

"Never leave home without your credit card?" one wit suggested.

There's no doubt a credit card is a handy thing to have, but even they have limits. What we really need is an "account" we can draw from at any time and where our credit is always good.

For many teenagers this will be the Bank of Mum and Dad. For the rest of us it's the Bank of Our Father Who Art In Heaven.

## Monday — June 18

A SOUTH AFRICAN pastor was visiting England in 1895. He was popular and had a lot of speaking engagements. In the midst of it all he heard of a woman who was too ill to come to hear him. He took a sheet of paper from his pocket and asked that it be sent to her.

What he had written there isn't important. The point is, while travelling, an old back injury had flared up, leaving him in a lot of pain. The notes on that sheet of paper were ones he had written to encourage himself. So, he knew they would help her.

Sometimes that is the point of our trials and troubles; that we might know better how to help someone else in a similar situation.

## Tuesday — June 19

I'M sure we have all heard the wise words, "It doesn't matter if you fall, what matters is that you get back up again."

The legendary jazz trumpeter and band-leader Miles Davis put a peculiarly musical twist on the notion when he said, "If you hit a wrong note, it's the next note that makes it good or bad."

In other words, don't be too rigid, leave room for mistakes, and be prepared to adapt. If you fall down with a crash, turn it into a drum roll.

## Wednesday — June 20

I HAD just heard for the first time what is apparently a really old saying – "When the gorse is out of bloom, kissing is out of season."

I recalled the last time I had smelled the sweet coconut and vanilla aroma of the gorse in bloom. Surely it had been in the spring. But I hadn't noticed any lack of blossom on those thorny bushes recently.

In some concern I turned to my nearest horticultural expert (or at least, keen gardener), Harry. I explained my upset. He started to sigh wearily at another of my annoying questions and then, on seeing my concern, he grinned.

"Have you never seen those yellow flowers peeking out from under the snow?" he asked. "Round about here, anyway, gorse is always in bloom. So, kissing is always . . ."

I may have to apologise for my rudeness in turning away so abruptly. At least I threw a thank-you over my shoulder as I left. But I suddenly found I had some jolly good news to share with the Lady of the House.

## Thursday — June 21

THE Reverend Gilbert White was a "parson-naturalist." In his walks about the parish in the late 18th century he observed and noted a wealth of detail concerning the wildlife who lived there. Such was his concern and interest in the birds and animals of his district that, after his death, his admirers created Britain's first bird sanctuary in his memory.

Reading through his journals, I was, in turn, educated and amazed by his observations and his understanding. But I looked particularly for entries concerning a certain hedgehog. After a parishioner died the Reverend was considerate enough to take her hibernating hedgehog to his own house and take care of it. Which tells you all you need to know about the man.

But the hedgehog entries among the detailed notes and accurate records told me something more. All the knowledge in the world is worth nothing if it is not, eventually, put towards the care of some person or some little creature.

## Friday — June 22

THE Wayland Smithy in Oxfordshire isn't actually a smithy. It is a restored stone-age burial site, surrounded, in part now, by standing stones. The name Wayland has connections with blacksmithing and legend has it that if you leave your horse there overnight, along with a silver coin, your horse will be shod by the morning. That would be something to be thankful for.

Or we could simply admire the craftsmanship of the tomb and be thankful for having a horse and a silver coin. I know I would be!

## Saturday — June 23

*DEAR Lord I'll really do my best,*
*I know you've put me to the test,*
*Help me use this day for you,*
*Filled with love in all I do.*
*Keep me smiling, filled with hope,*
*Strong and healthy, so I'll cope,*
*And never grumble, patient be,*
*Only kind and gentle me,*
*Then when the day is turned to night,*
*I'll be at peace – I did things right!*

– Chrissy Greenslade.

## Sunday — June 24

ARE you looking after your little brother?" the checkout operator asked. The three-year-old gave the baby's pram a little shake and said, "Yes! It's a full-time job and I'm getting fed up with it."

Meanwhile, her mother, who handled all the real responsibilities in the little girl's life, mostly without her knowing anything about them, smiled indulgently.

I couldn't help but imagine Our Father on high, smiling the same loving, knowing smile when we grown-up children complain about all we have to do.

## Monday — June 25

**DOROTHY DAY** was an American social reformer, not a gardener. But she mixed both the disciplines wonderfully when she wrote these words – "We plant seeds that will flower as results in our lives. So, best to remove the weeds of anger, avarice, envy and doubt, so that peace and abundance may manifest for all."

Have you any weeding to do? I know I have!

## Tuesday — June 26

**DAME MARGOT FONTEYN** was one of the world's greatest prima donnas, in the original meaning of being the "first lady" of the ballet company.

But the term has another meaning these days. Prima donnas are sometimes women (and men) who want everything their way and make a big fuss if they don't get what they want.

I have no idea how difficult Dame Margot was to work with; how much like that second sort of prima donna she was.

But a clue to that might be in these words of hers we might apply equally well to whatever it is we do.

"Take your work seriously, but never yourself."

## Wednesday — June 27

**NATURE'S** bounty is free and much is given to us for love – but sometimes we appreciate it more and it tastes a little sweeter if we have to put some effort into it.

As in this description of a fine walk by the English art critic and essayist William Hazlitt.

"Give me the clear blue sky over my head, and the green turf beneath my feet, a winding road before me, and three hours' march before dinner."

Oh, how satisfying that walked-for meal would be! Of course, it also helps to have someone making your dinner . . .

## Thursday — June 28

*IT doesn't cost a penny, it doesn't cost a dime,*
*Yet, on show, there is no doubt, it's stood the test of time.*
*It doesn't cost a rouble, a euro or a yen,*
*Yet it has been with us since I don't know when,*
*The dividend's enormous, yet the cost of it is nil,*
*And all it takes to use it is what is called goodwill.*
*So, when next you see a stranger, simply pause a while,*
*And with no hesitation, give them a great big smile . . .*

– Brian H. Gent.

## Friday — June 29

THE man had come into the foodbank without the required reference and with a slightly ridiculous story. A few minutes later he walked out with a food parcel.

"Weren't you worried he was taking advantage of you?" I asked Craig, who organised the thing.

"He might have been," Craig replied. "Or he might not. But I would rather be fooled a dozen times than turn away one genuinely hungry person because I was too cynical."

Kindness and humility like that are truly food for my soul.

## Saturday — June 30

IT was his second night on the streets. The first night he just walked and kept walking. The second night he found a bench by the sea-front. He didn't sleep, but he sat there. When I suggested that would have been a long night he told me how he had passed the time – counting his blessings!

After getting him a room in a hostel I returned home to my own warm and cosy bed, determined to be more appreciative. I might have stayed awake all night counting blessings as he had, if the under-appreciated blessing of safe and comfortable sleep hadn't taken me away first. I was very thankful for that!

# July

A FAMILY took their three-year-old son on his first trip to the beach. He was really excited and looking forward to playing with his bucket and spade. It took them a couple of hours to get from their home to the resort. But it took them almost as long to get from the resort car park to the shore, a distance of a few hundred yards.

Every time the boy came to a patch of sand on the path, he insisted on stopping and playing as if this was the beach he had heard so much about. They had to keep telling him there was bigger and better to come. He had no comprehension of the size of the beach, let alone the ocean.

Our lives will be full of diversions and distractions that look quite heavenly, and we can spend time there, but we should never forget what the Bible reminds us of – that there is much bigger and better to come.

I DO enjoy looking through old newspapers and magazines, not so much for the current affairs as for how people lived their lives.

Some might have smiled at the sight of me on the library computer perusing "The Ladies' Pocket Magazine" from the 1830s, but I couldn't resist their Advice to Young Ladies.

There were comments on eye colour and pretty feet, the length of petticoats, which type of hands were best for tapestry and which for playing the harp.

But the last three suggestions struck me as being important for men *and* women, even in these modern times.

- If you would preserve esteem, be gentle
- If you would obtain power, first have humility
- And if you would live happily, endeavour to promote the happiness of others.

## Tuesday — July 3

KNOW a minister who can turn almost anything into a sermon.

He was breaking up some wood in his garden when he slipped and landed hard on his rear end. When the shock of the impact wore off he realised he had also landed on a piece of wood. The nail sticking out of it had smoothly slid through his trousers and pierced his "dignity."

He didn't realise what had happened at first, but when he did . . . oh, boy!

So, how did that become a sermon?

"It's like sin," he told the congregation. "You hardly notice it slip into your life. But it's a painful process getting it out again!"

## Wednesday — July 4

JAMES FENIMORE COOPER, who wrote "The Last Of The Mohicans", knew a thing or two about life in the woods and mountains. And he noticed that even in the coldest part of winter, with snow thick on the ground, the water from underground streams still flowed unfrozen. This was because it had been protected from the worst of the weather by the insulating earth.

In a charming comparison he added that, likewise, "Friendship that flows from the heart cannot be frozen by adversity."

## Thursday — July 5

HARRIET TUBMAN was the founder of the so-called Underground Railroad in the United States. She helped countless men and women escape slavery in the south and get to the freedom of the northern states. They depended on her for their lives. But she, in turn, depended on someone else.

At the beginning of each "run" she is said to have told God, "I'm going to hold steady on to you, an' you've got to see me through."

Despite having a reward on her head, Harriet Tubman and the Underground Railroad never lost a "passenger". The One she held on to always saw her through to the end of the journey.

Pretty in pink.

## Friday — July 6

THE boulder was large enough for my legs to dangle. I had no demands on my time. The sun glinted off the stream and I could hear the water laugh as it tumbled over the rocks.

Boughs laden with greenery swayed gently before me. A breeze warmed my skin. I closed my eyes.

And, in the background, some happy young men sang vulgar and raucous football chants.

Ah, well, if I'd had too much of heaven in the one day I might never have gone back to "normal" life!

## Saturday — July 7

IF you set yourself a goal in life, first make sure it is one worth pursuing, one worth giving your all for. I take as my example C.S. Lewis's creation Reepicheep the mouse, who was absolutely determined to journey east in search of Aslan the lion. This was how he put it.

"While I may, I sail east in the *Dawn Treader*. When she fails me, I row east in my coracle. When that sinks, I shall paddle east with my four paws. Then, when I can swim no longer, if I have not yet reached Aslan's country, there shall I sink with my nose to the sunrise."

Choose your goals wisely. Then give them your all.

## Sunday — July 8

AMRIT VELA, in Sikh tradition, is the time before dawn, when the world is just thinking about waking. This is the time that the devout spend alone with God in preparation for the day ahead and whatever it may bring.

Putting some "God-time" between you and the day ahead isn't just a Sikh practice; it is something people of faith have done for centuries.

Whether it's before dawn, or before leaving your bedroom, it's the best possible way to start the day.

## Monday — July 9

DO you have a friendship in your life where it doesn't matter how long you go without seeing each other, you just pick right up where you left off? It's a wonderful thing and it leaves me in delighted awe when it happens.

But I never thought to question it – until the Lady of the House explained it to me.

"Friendship," she said, in that familiar patient but loving tone, "isn't measured in time spent. It's measured in time spent together. It's different, do you see?"

And I did!

## Tuesday — July 10

DO we still have vocational guidance advisors at school? The difference between them and careers advice officers might be nothing in practice, but there is a difference in the words.

A career is something you can spend a lifetime working at, a vocation is something you were called to be or something you feel a strong suitability for.

I had to smile at the idea of Therese of Lisieux taking on the role. Apart from the fact that she lived long before modern schools were thought of, she would most likely have given the one piece of advice to all her students – "Love is the vocation which includes all others."

## Wednesday — July 11

FOR those young sweethearts about to take the matrimonial plunge this summer – and for those older sweethearts who did it long ago – here is an ancient marriage prayer that must surely guarantee a happy ever after.

"May we two live our lives so happily together that God will enjoy our union of hearts and spirits."

Imagine . . . that you could be so romantic you would make even heaven smile. It's possible!

## Thursday — July 12

THERE'S a little island somewhere near Greenland that is disputed territory. Both the Canadian and the Danish governments claim Hans Island and the dispute has been rumbling on for decades. Every few years the navy of one or other side will land sailors there to take down the other country's flag and fly their own.

Politically, it might be a serious issue, but I hear the sailors have their own way of lightening the situation. When the Danes take down a flag they leave a bottle of schnapps for the Canadians they know will be along shortly. The Canadian sailors return the favour with a bottle of whisky.

Now, there's a way to deal with disputes, be they international or neighbourly. Stake your claim, but be polite and never forget to extend your hospitality as well.

## Friday — July 13

MARY OLIVER, one of the best-selling poets in the world, asked, "What does it mean that the world is so beautiful? And what shall I do about it?"

Some people choose to see the world as a depressing place because that lets them off the hook. Nothing can be done.

But if the world is beautiful (and I am sure you and I agree that it is) then Ms Oliver's question remains. And the only sensible answers are, preserve it, enjoy it, add to it!

## Saturday — July 14

IF ever you visit Batemans, the house once owned by Rudyard Kipling and now cared for by the National Trust, you might notice some unusual initials in the visitors' book.

*FIP* after your name means that you fell in the pond. The pond that Kipling built is shallow, ornamental and easily seen. It is unlikely to take anyone by surprise, so the most likely reason for falling in would be over-reaching or being too adventurous; traits that Kipling, author of many tales of adventure, would surely approve of.

**New horizons.**

*Dover's white cliffs, England.*

## Sunday — July 15

NOBODY likes waste. Or so they say.

Theologian Paul Tillich had a different opinion. He talked about "holy waste," as in the times we give too much, or go further than is sensible to help someone. Examples of holy waste in the Bible are when the woman anointed Jesus with expensive perfume, or Joseph of Arimathea giving away his personal tomb, or when the woman washed Jesus's feet with her tears.

A sensible balance is important in life, but let us not always be sensible. From time to time be willing to waste yourself or your resources, not in self-indulgence, but in the cause of love.

Nobody likes waste – but God is very fond of a little holy waste.

## Monday — July 16

THERE'S a video doing the rounds of the internet where a man tells of how his grandad copes with life after the death of his wife. Grandad, striking out on his own, is amazed at the help he is offered and is full of appreciation.

The younger man asks how he always seems to see the glass as half full instead of half empty. Grandad stops, thinks for a moment, and says, "It's a beautiful glass!"

Happily, I can add nothing to that!

## Tuesday — July 17

JAMES had struggled for years with various issues and, at last, had overcome them. He shared the thoughts that had made such a positive difference. And I remembered telling him these things a year ago! Had they lain dormant until the time came for them to grow?

I was reminded of it by the words of the 19th-century poet Celia Laighton Thaxter, who wrote, "The very act of planting a seed in the earth has in it, to me, something beautiful. I always do it with a joy that is largely mixed with awe."

Planting a seed is always a wonderful thing – whether it is an actual seed or an encouraging word.

## Wednesday — July 18

AMERICAN President Theodore Roosevelt once said, "Comparison is the thief of joy." It's a good quote – but not as good as some by Lincoln, or Kennedy, or . . .

Do you see what he meant? If I had settled for saying, "It's a good quote," then all would have been fine, but the comparison with other Presidents took the joy right out of it all, making it seem less than it actually was.

We do this in so many aspects of life, comparing holidays with other holidays, meals with other meals, ourselves with other people.

If we would have more joy in our lives let's ditch the comparisons and appreciate the thing, the moment and the person for all they themselves are worth.

As words of wisdom go, I am tempted to say these are better than most, and not as good as others – but I wouldn't want to rob them of their joy!

## Thursday — July 19

I REMEMBER a primary school teacher drawing the outline of a Viking longboat on the blackboard. The chalk went down at an angle then across the board in what seemed to me to be the most beautifully drawn horizontal free-hand line.

I remember standing on a bridge over a motorway and being entranced by the beauty of electricity pylons silhouetted against a sunset. I remember the appreciation in the face of a woman I gave some change to a decade ago, though she never said a word in reply.

Why am I talking about these things; these things that took me aback at the time and are as fresh in my mind now as they ever were?

It's partly because I want to ask if you have any moments like them; times when you were unexpectedly captivated by seemingly mundane things of this world. And partly because of these words by the art historian Sister Wendy Beckett.

"The eye that sees nobility and beauty in what another would regard as ordinary is the eye of prayer."

## Friday — July 20

*SOMETIMES things can happen which cause sadness, shock and
 pain,
They make us stop and wonder if we can face life again.
But deep inside God's power brings us strength and helps us
 through,
We're guided in so many ways in everything we do.
When we're confused and weary but we know we've tried our best
We'll keep our faith, then we will find that God will do the rest,
For as His power's within us, we can turn our lives around,
And find a new beginning where fresh hope and love abound.
We'll face whatever happens, knowing that support is near,
With courage and acceptance, doubt and fear will disappear.
For hope and positivity will fill our days with light,
And we will find that, after all, the future's looking bright.*
                                                    – Chrissy Greenslade.

## Saturday — July 21

DO you need more space in your life? No, I'm not suggesting you
declutter your home! The Austrian psychiatrist and concentration
camp survivor Viktor Frankl talked about the space between the
thing that happens to us and how we respond. For better or worse
we respond automatically. But Frankl suggested that in that space
we might think about responding differently, and that more positive
responses might make our future happier and healthier.

So, ask yourself . . . do you need more space in your life?

## Sunday — July 22

PEOPLE love to offer definitions of life. I have heard some good,
bad and indifferent opinions of what it's all about. But my
favourite comes from inspirational speaker Corrie ten Boom.

"The measure of a life is not its duration, but its donation."

After all, we are given these lives. How better to use them than by
giving them away to as many other people in as many positive ways
as we can?

## Monday — July 23

DENNY is a do-it-yourself kind of guy. And usually he does just fine on his own. But recently health problems and other situations have conspired to make him more dependent. Wonderfully, the results of all that were actually positive differences in his life. But he did have to admit that the differences weren't down to him.

"It's OK," he told me. "I don't mind being humbled. In fact, I'm pretty great at being humble."

A little humility will take you a long way in this life. And so will a sense of humour.

## Tuesday — July 24

I LIKED Nigel almost immediately, which struck me as odd because he hadn't really said more than a few words.

It puzzled me for a while and then I realised – it was the accent. I know another fellow from the same area and he is, in my opinion, one of the kindest, humblest, most patient and understanding people I have ever met.

So, when I met someone who sounded like him, I unconsciously assumed they would be like him.

Nigel also turned out to be a lovely man. But it reminded me that how we live our lives can have far-reaching effects we never imagine.

## Wednesday — July 25

BEING a scientist doesn't mean you can't also be poetic. Rachel Carson, a biologist in the mid-1900s, wasn't intending to be poetic when she wrote the following, but I think she managed it anyway.

"Those who contemplate the beauty of the earth," she wrote, "find reserves of strength that will endure as long as life lasts. There is symbolic and actual beauty in the migration of the birds, the ebb and flow of the tides, the folded bud ready for spring. There is something infinitely healing in the repeated refrains of nature – the assurance that dawn comes after night, and spring after the winter."

## Thursday — July 26

PEOPLE talk about counting their blessings. The English poet Elizabeth Jennings was talking of something similar when she wrote – "I count the moments of my mercies up. I make a list of love and find it full. I do all this before I sleep."

What a wonderful way to end the day; before you sleep to spend a few minutes adding up every moment of kindness, grace and love you experienced or shared in that day.

Falling asleep in a spirit of gratitude almost guarantees the next day will have more of the same.

## Friday — July 27

RICHARD ROLLE was a 14th-century English hermit who rather spoiled the image by constantly being sought out for his advice. His meditations spilled out in copious writings which were first laid down in Latin. The appreciation of his wisdom was such that it went beyond the learned classes and he started writing in ordinary English.

A thought of his that we might make good use of was given in response to a query from someone about a third person's character. "If thou wilt ask, 'How good is he or she?'" he replied, "ask, 'how much loves he or she?'"

I can think of no better way to get the true measure of someone.

## Saturday — July 28

AT the risk of seeming immature, it occurred to me that St Basil – with a name like that – might know a thing or two about herbs. Nonsense, of course, although many of the monks of his day did grow their own food, and it turns out he did know a thing or two about gardening.

"He who sows courtesy," he wrote, "reaps friendship. And he who plants kindness gathers love."

Not traditional farming methods, of course, but still raising crops worth having. Wouldn't you agree?

## Sunday — July 29

RENDERED in everyday English, Ephrem's Prayer asks God to keep us from being indifferent or discouraged, to keep us from wasting time in idle chatter or chasing after influence. Instead it asks God to grant humility, wholeness, patience and love.

It is about seventeen centuries old and was written by Ephrem the Syrian. He lived when the Roman Empire was being attacked from the east, and he died of plague after ministering to sufferers.

Very different times and a different life from what most of us will have experienced, but couldn't each of us apply those principles to our lives today? Ephrem's Prayer reminds us that the essentials today are the same as they were back then. The same as they always have been.

## Monday — July 30

HARRY fights a running battle with dandelions in his garden. But despite the frustration they cause him, he has a sneaking regard for the little weeds and thinks more people should be like them.

Of course, I had to ask why.

"Well, they're persistent, for one thing," he said. "They seem to have no other purpose than to delight children, they don't limit their appearances to where others think they ought to be, and they always present a cheery face."

And when it's all over, I thought, they take to the wind ready to do more of the same next year.

## Tuesday — July 31

THE avant garde musician John Cage rather famously "composed" a piece called "4.33." It was, of course, four minutes and thirty-three seconds of complete silence.

Some people thought it a brave, ground-breaking composition. Others ridiculed it. Which side do you come down on?

And might it change your opinion if you knew it was originally called "A Silent Prayer"?

# August

B ACK when I was learning to drive, my uncle would occasionally tell me to leave the steering to him while he demonstrated a lighter touch or had me focus on the pedals.

The first time I almost had to peel my fingers from the steering wheel. After we did it a few times without crashes I grew much more blasé about it. These days, of course, I keep both hands firmly on the wheel.

I thought about those times as I read these words by the singer Gloria Gaither.

"With each new experience of letting God be in control we gain courage and reinforcement for daring to do it again and again."

So, when things in your life need a finer touch, or your attention must of necessity be elsewhere, let God take the wheel for a while. He will never steer you wrong.

## Thursday — August 2

T HE air-show was in full flight. Powerful jets blasted the runway, propeller planes painted the sky with coloured smoke, the latest fighters showed breathtaking agility; an awe-inspiring reminder of how far mankind has come in a century of flight.

But from her seat in the stands Evie was distracted by the chirping of a sparrow.

It hopped off the top of the chain-link fence, turned, flew to the fence, retracted its wings at the last second and flew through the little diamond-shaped gap, spreading those wings as it cleared the wire. Then it turned and repeated the manoeuvre . . . and again, and again.

"Now, I'm not saying this was God saying, 'Look what I can do'," Evie told me with a grin. Then she added, "But I'm not saying it wasn't, either!"

Come and play!

## Friday — August 3

I KNOW some people who don't enjoy the company of cheerful people. When pushed they might say they think such cheerfulness can't be anything but fake.

Maybe they are afraid, afraid that the cheerful ones will ask something of them, attracting some inner part of them that secretly believes in better and wants to rise to the challenge.

Most of us, though, enjoy the company of cheerful people, coming away from the encounter refreshed and uplifted. But let us not simply be takers. Let us be givers also, being, from time to time, the cheerful one who uplifts others, being especially gentle with our grumpier brothers and sisters, but not neglecting them.

## Saturday — August 4

THE Greek philosopher and mathematician Pythagoras would not be counted as a friend by the schoolchildren who struggled to learn his theorem regarding triangles.

But he did have some interesting thoughts on friendship.

"Friends," he wrote, "are as companions on a journey, aiding each other to persevere along the road to a happier life."

Now, if only he would be a friend and aid me to remember what the square of the hypotenuse is equal to!

## Sunday — August 5

MANY will know, and have been inspired by, the Apostle's Creed. Cecil Frances Alexander was perhaps inspired more than most.

The line, "I believe in God the Father, the Almighty, maker of heaven and earth," moved her to write "All Things Bright And Beautiful". The part about Jesus's conception by the Holy Spirit prompted her to write "Once In Royal David's City." The part about Christ's crucifixion was the spur to create "There Is a Green Hill Far Away."

All that (and more) from the Apostle's Creed! Devotion often turns to inspiration, if we only delve deep enough.

## Monday — August 6

BACK in the ninth century an unknown poet crafted "The Sea-farer". It tells how the coming of spring urges the traveller who has stayed put all winter to venture forth. Even while he is still at home, the poet asserts, the sea-farer's spirit is actually out there on the oceans, feeling the warmth of the sun as he sails beneath the gull and above the whale.

He ends by declaring it is the same for those of us who are "wintering" in this world with souls that long for another.

"And in the same way, to me, the joys of the Lord are warmer than this life lent on the land."

## Tuesday — August 7

THE 1957 movie "An Affair To Remember" was part of the inspiration for the more recent "Sleepless In Seattle". It also contains the scene where Deborah Kerr asks Cary Grant, "What makes life so difficult?"

His reply is one emphatic word: "People!" Obviously his character's experience of people had been a frustrating one.

But people are also what make life wonderful. All we need is for everyone to remember that when faced with some of its more challenging personalities!

## Wednesday — August 8

I THINK these words might equally apply to any kind of success worth having in life – but Arnold Schwarzenegger, erstwhile Governor of California, Hollywood superstar and professional body-builder, says they apply to strength. He should know – and I'm not going to argue with him!

"Strength does not come from winning. Your struggles develop your strengths. When you go through hardships and decide not to surrender, that is strength."

Keeping going; it's how we use our strength and where we find it that's important.

## Thursday — August 9

SARAH knelt to pray. She had been asked to help a starving family in Romania. She knew she could get them sponsored, but it would take a month. And they didn't have a month. She calculated how much it would cost to feed and shelter them for a month, then she humbly asked her Father for it.

Thousands of miles away, Davie had just received a large cheque and felt an urge to donate 10% to Sarah (whom he had never met) for her charitable work.

The amount he sent? The same as she asked for. The time he felt that urge? The same time Sarah knelt to pray.

## Friday — August 10

JOHN posted a photo of the riverbank he was sitting by on social media. He added that Ella Fitzgerald was singing "Summertime" in his earphones, Louis Armstrong was on trumpet, and he was enjoying a lunch prepared by someone who loved him.

"It's like being in heaven," he said. "What did I do to deserve this?"

There were several replies. Someone said he was lucky to have been born where he was. Someone else suggested he was luckier to have a wife who made his lunch. Then a friend gave the definitive answer.

"You learned how to appreciate."

## Saturday — August 11

US Secretary of Defence Donald Rumsfeld once said, "There are known knowns – these are things that we know we know. There are known unknowns – the things that we know we don't know. But there are also unknown unknowns – these are things we don't know we don't know."

The known knowns and the known unknowns pretty much sum up ordinary life for most of us. But once we understand there are unknown unknowns all around us – and they are working for the best – then life becomes a whole lot more wonderful.

## Sunday — August 12

JOY. It's a good word, but somehow, a little soft. Not the most powerful emotion, perhaps.

Janet Erskine Stuart, an English nun and educator who died in 1914, had a different take.

"To be a joy-bearer and a joy-giver says everything," she wrote. "For in our life if one is joyful it means that one is faithfully living for God. And if one gives joy to others one is doing God's work. With joy without and joy within, all is well. I can conceive no higher way."

## Monday — August 13

HUMAN beings are creatures of habit. So, is that a good thing or a bad thing?

Elisabeth Elliot, whose husband was killed while working as a missionary in South America, and who later went back to forgive and work with the tribespeople who killed him, had this to say.

"It is always possible to be thankful for what is given rather to complain about what is not given. One or the other becomes a habit for life."

So is it a good thing or a bad thing? It depends on the choice we make.

## Tuesday — August 14

J.N.W. SULLIVAN was a popular science writer in London in the early 1900s. But he looked at the world with more than just a scientific eye.

He wrote about the times he saw the world with fresh eyes, the times the ordinary seems spectacular. Once, in the right light, an ivy-covered wall was so beautiful to him it moved him to tears.

The question he asked was, was he seeing the things differently – or more deeply. He believed that those wonderful moments were actually a more profound understanding of the wonder of creation. And he believed it was possible to see people in the same way.

So do I.

## Wednesday — August 15

IF you want to see boats, go uphill and visit the Caen Hill locks in Wiltshire.

Canal locks need a "basin" of water to enable them to work. Normally the basin is incorporated into the canal itself, but at Caen Hill the sixteen locks needed to be so close together there was no space for basin stretches. So the engineer John Rennie placed his basins out to the side of the main canal.

Sometimes, when your problems make life seem like a never-ending steep hill, a little sideways thinking can be the key to unlocking your difficulties.

## Thursday — August 16

FRIENDS! Some people have lots of them and seem to acquire them easily. Some have a few and would be lost without them. Some seem to manage quite well without any, but, if truth be told . . .

Well, I can think of no "non-essential" thing the majority of us want more, whether we admit it or not.

Ralph Waldo Emerson described the urge towards friendship beautifully when he wrote, "A friend is the hope of the heart."

Every heart, I believe.

## Friday — August 17

IN the lazy summer days where (if we are lucky) we notice the sounds of the natural world more, my mind drifts to Rob Angus, a woodworker and creation of J.M. Barrie.

When Rob found himself charged with caring for a baby and needing to work he crafted a cradle with paddles, sat it across a stream and let the water rock the bairn to sleep.

Water tumbling over stones, the distant buzz of a bee about its work, the singing of the birds.

We are more attuned to nature than we sometimes care to admit. And I feel a nap coming on!

*THE path of life has twists and turns,*
*Who knows what's round the bend?*
*And who knows what tomorrow holds,*
*Or what today will send?*

*The path of life climbs up the hills,*
*The way is often steep,*
*But many times the sun breaks through*
*With memories to keep.*

*Then from the hilltop see the view,*
*It's better than before.*
*That distant, bright horizon shines*
*And helps our spirits soar.*

*Be brave through all the twists and turns*
*Whatever comes along,*
*The path leads on to hope and joy,*
*Go cheerfully, be strong!*

– Iris Hesselden.

## Sunday — August 19

ABOUT a century and a half ago the *SS Great Eastern* set about laying telegraph cables from Porthcurno in Cornwall out into the immensity of the Atlantic Ocean, all so that headquarters in London could be able to communicate with every corner of the British Empire.

Another immensity separates heaven and Earth and yet, paradoxically, it is no distance at all.

We can send messages there any time we like; no ships or cables required.

We can even talk while we are sitting on the clifftop at Porthcurno (or any other place for that matter) and we can be sure in the knowledge that the message will be received at our heavenly headquarters.

Fragrant field.

*Lavender field, southern France.*

## Monday — August 20

IT'S just like a poet to take something most people never notice and make it beautiful – or perhaps reveal a previously unsuspected truth!

Hildegard of Bingen, the 11th-century German nun and poet, had this to say about something that surrounds us all – "Just so, the breath of the air makes the earth fruitful. The air is the soul of the earth, moistening it, greening it."

Rise early on a spring morning and stand in the garden or in a park and see if you don't agree.

## Tuesday — August 21

WE are generally told that extravagance is a bad thing. And I generally agree – in everything except love.

The writer Joni Eareckson Tada described love as being "extravagant in the price it is willing to pay, the time it is willing to give, the hardships it is willing to endure, and the strength it is willing to spend."

Love never thinks in terms of "how little" but always in terms of "how much".

As with every rule there is an exception. Be frugal in all things. But be extravagant in love!

## Wednesday — August 22

*BUSY people always seem*
*The ones who understand*
*Someone else's problems,*
*And find time to lend a hand.*
*Yes, we all have problems,*
*But life has often shown*
*By overcoming others' woes*
*We overcome our own!*

– Elizabeth Gozney.

## Thursday — August 23

THE most impressive display of strength I ever saw wasn't in any strongman competition. It came from a wee woman, not much over five feet tall, who told me that her family seemed to be falling apart.

She listed their many and various troubles, then said, "But I won't let it fall apart."

On the verge of tears, she stretched her arms wide and added, "Not while I can wrap these around them and hold the family together."

Now, that's real strength. That's real love!

## Friday — August 24

HOW would you like to dance through your days? Oh, I hear you say, but life can be hard; too hard for dancing.

Laura Ingalls Wilder, as one of the family who inspired the "Little House On The Prairie" television series, knew about how hard life could be. Out there on the frontier everyone worked, even the children.

But she wrote these thought-provoking words: "Life is not intended to be simply a round of work. A moment's pause to watch the glory of a sunrise or a sunset is soul satisfying, while a bird's song will set the steps to music all day long."

And what are steps set to music but dancing?

## Saturday — August 25

THE old gypsy woman was selling trinkets door to door. We talked for a moment about her way of life and how for every friendly response she met with someone would be rude or slam the door in her face. I asked how she coped, being on the receiving end of such behaviour day after day.

"Oh, I just pray for them as I walk on," she said.

I wondered after she left – if they knew her response, might those poor souls be less grumpy?

## Sunday — August 26

AFTER the longest ever term in office, the US President Franklin Delano Roosevelt had these words inscribed on the fireplace in the State Dining-room.

"I pray to heaven to bestow the best of blessings on this house and on all that shall hereafter inhabit it. May none but honest and wise men ever rule under this roof."

A wonderful thought to leave behind and one we might take into our own homes, whether they are "ruled" by a man or a woman, and whether we have a stately fireplace or a three-bar heater.

May we be blessed, honest and wise.

## Monday — August 27

A STORY is told of the Welsh poet George Herbert. He was on his way to band practice with friends one day when he stopped along the way to help a man whose cart had fallen on him. Arriving dishevelled, and telling the story, his friends suggested he had sullied his dignity.

In response he told them that helping the other man had provided music for his own soul that would play long after the act.

Then, in a fine touch of wry humour, he suggested they all retune their instruments.

## Tuesday — August 28

I DO like the Gaelic tradition of *anam cara*. "Anam" means "soul" and "cara" means "friend." A "soul-friend" in times gone by was often a teacher or spiritual advisor.

But these days it means the kind of friend you were always destined to be with. The one who understands – and shares – your lows and your highs.

The question is, can you become an *anam cara*, or is it in fact a pre-destined thing? Who knows? Well, it is a wonderful thing to aim for, surely. We lose nothing by trying and may gain a soul-friend in the process.

Winding road.

*Carrick-a-Rede Rope Bridge,*
*County Antrim, Northern Ireland.*

## Wednesday — August 29

PAMELA timed it just right. She had been talking to one of the church's summer groups about saints. So, at the right time, she brought the children from the back hall into the sanctuary just as the sun lit up the stained-glass tableau.

Then she delivered the punch-line: "Saints are the ones who let the Light of God shine through them!"

All very wonderful. And George seemed to think so as well. He had just cleaned the windows and waited patiently for Pamela to finish before tidying up after himself.

Sometimes, I thought, saints are the humble servants who make it possible for the Light to be seen to best effect.

## Thursday — August 30

CHA SA-SOON was a Korean woman who wanted to learn to drive a car. Getting the money together for lessons was extremely difficult and she took three attempts at sitting her test. Oh, and she was sixty-nine when she started the process. But she did get her licence. Why did she bother? Because she wanted to be able to take her great-granddaughter to the zoo.

There is very little we can't do – if we have someone we love enough to do it for!

## Friday — August 31

HOW would you like to achieve something meaningful for world peace?

That's all very well, you might say, but if you're not a politician or world leader what can you do that would make a difference?

You could take the advice of Mahatma Gandhi, who said, "With every true friendship we build more firmly the foundations on which the peace of the whole world rests."

Be a true friend. Peace will come to your part of the world. Then it's up to everyone else to follow your fine example. One friendship at a time, peace will grow and spread.

# September

## Saturday — September 1

AFTER a night out with friends George found himself walking down a dark, secluded lane towards the railway station. Half-jokingly, he started praying for a Guardian Angel. Then he saw a figure approaching him out of the gloom.

The large, menacing figure stopped, and said, "Grandad?"

George's grandson had also been on a night out, had spent his fare home and hadn't been able to get his parents on the phone. He'd been walking along the scary path to a friend's house when he also had seen a "menacing figure".

George walked him back to the station, bought his ticket, and saw him safely home.

"I asked God for a Guardian Angel," George said, laughing. "And He sent me for my grandson! But, sometimes, that's how it works."

## Sunday — September 2

DON'T worry yet awhile." The fourth-century bishop John Chrysostom offered this advice on dealing with trying times.

A farmer collected grain – and then locked it away in a barn! Later the same farmer casually tossed the grain to the wind, leaving it in the dirt, then walked away and apparently forgot about it.

Surely, from the grain's point of view it had been taken from home, imprisoned, and then abandoned. But the farmer knew more than the grain, and the man who watched and wondered. He had sunny days and waving fields of tall corn in mind.

"Now, if the farmer waits all winter," Chrysostom wrote, "how much more ought we to wait, remembering who it is who ploughs the soil of our souls?"

Don't worry yet awhile. God has the bigger picture.

## Monday — September 3

I WON'T embarrass the local council by naming the town, but some locals were so fed up with the potholes in their roads that they filled them with dirt and put flowers in them. The publicity these impromptu gardens attracted meant the potholes were quickly repaired.

But for a little while those stretches of tarmac (while perhaps not being very safe) actually looked quite attractive.

It occurred to me that it really doesn't take much to make our built-up areas nice; just some motived souls, some seeds and some dirt. Look around and see if there's something you and your friends could do. But let's stay out of the traffic while we are prettying the place up!

## Tuesday — September 4

IN her diary, Great-aunt Louisa suggested there was an art, or a ritual, to getting ready for bed.

"When I wash," she wrote, "Lord, make it a holy sacrament that it may cleanse the inner woman, removing my grievances against Mrs . . . and wiping away my anger at that ridiculous Miss . . . And, as I am weary, do Thou pitch my weariness through the window and gather up all the day's good under my pillow. Teach me to go to sleep with a lovely thought in my mind, that it might grow in the night and blossom in the dawn, so I may rise in the morning with its fragrance everywhere about me."

## Wednesday — September 5

WHICH is your favourite season? Personally, I like the time when one season (whichever season it is) changes into the next.

French journalist Maurice Chapelan had a different take. He wrote – "I love the spring mornings, the afternoons in autumn, the winter evenings, and the summer nights."

We might have our favourites, but every season has its delights. Let's not miss one pining for another.

## Thursday — September 6

*HAPPINESS held is only a seed,*
*Happiness needs to be shared,*
*Swiftly it spreads and touches more souls*
*Showing how somebody cared.*
*Happiness shared is a flower,*
*Blooming in darkness or light,*
*Growing so strong, its roots reaching out*
*Its colours so glowing and bright.*
*Happiness held is only a seed,*
*Don't keep it or store it away,*
*Reach out to others and share what you have*
*And it will return every day!*

– Iris Hesselden.

## Friday — September 7

IN Peter Pan, J.M. Barrie suggested that after children fell asleep mothers rummaged among their thoughts, tidying them, stowing the darker ones away, and laying out bright, fresh thoughts for the children to dress their minds with in the morning.

Wouldn't it be wonderful if, now we are grown up, we could learn to do likewise for ourselves? Days begun with bright thoughts will surely lead to a life with far fewer of the other kind to stow away.

## Saturday — September 8

A CERTAIN man is often made cross by foolishness. No doubt, to others, he seems grumpy. And now he is cross with that normally wise philosopher Friedrich Nietzsche for saying, "The growth of wisdom may be gauged exactly by the diminution of ill-temper."

Then there was the Frenchman, Michel de Montaigne, who wrote, "The most manifest sign of wisdom is a continual cheerfulness, a state like that in the regions above the moon, always clear and calm."

How could he be calm when they write such nonsense? (I never said I was wise anyway!)

## Sunday — September 9

DID you ever mis-hear something and go for years without being corrected?

I like these hymn titles as understood by children.

"We shall come to Joyce's, bringing in the cheese."

"Gladly the Cross-eyed Bear."

And the prayer, "Give us this day our deli bread."

Thankfully, God hears us correctly, because He listens to the prayer of our hearts. So, make sure your heart is saying the right thing, and the right words can come when they will.

## Monday — September 10

WHILE patents officer Charles Duell was saying everything that could be invented had been, Lucy Montgomery's character Anne of Green Gables was saying, "Isn't it splendid to think of all there is to find out about? It's such an interesting world. It wouldn't be half so interesting if we knew all about everything."

Both those opinions were expressed a century ago. Look how much the world has changed since then! Many scientists feel they are only at the beginning of their understanding of the universe.

What does it tell you that when we think we know it all there is more – much more – to learn?

It tells me we need never stop being amazed.

## Tuesday — September 11

THE author Franz Kafka was noted for his very serious but quite fantastical writing. So, I wondered, when I heard he had the secret to eternal youth, was this more fantasy?

Then I read it and decided he may well have stumbled on to something.

"Youth is happy," he wrote, "because it has the ability to see beauty. Anyone who keeps the ability to see beauty never grows old."

## Wednesday — September 12

LIFE! What's it all about?

Have you ever said that? You would think with the amount of people who have ever lived someone would have figured it out by now. And perhaps someone has!

The writer Oscar Wilde wrote, "All I know is that life cannot be understood without charity, cannot be lived without charity. It is love and not philosophy that is the true explanation of this world, whatever may be the explanation of the next."

What's it all about? Love! In this world and, I predict, in the next.

## Thursday — September 13

A MAN from long ago complained that every time he looked out his window he saw broken trees and bent people. What a miserable scene it was! So, he stayed indoors as much as possible.

Then came a storm that rattled his house and broke his window. Glass making had improved greatly since his house was built. The new panes were smooth and clear. And suddenly the trees were fine and the people noble in their bearing.

When we judge the world, as we do despite our best intentions, let's make sure we don't see it through the old glass of our misconceptions. Better still, go out into it and see it as it really is.

## Friday — September 14

IS there any such thing as the perfect married couple? Robert Louis Stevenson didn't think so, and he was a married man. What's more, he thought that was a good thing!

"The faults of married people," he wrote, "continually spur each of them, hour by hour, to do better, and to meet and love upon a higher ground. And ever, between the failures, there will come glimpses of kind virtues to encourage and console."

So, ever onwards, hand in hand, with all our faults, to that wonderful higher ground.

## Saturday — September 15

**READ** somewhere of a man who was part of an outreach mission, helping villagers in a poor country recover from some natural disaster. When it was time for them to leave a large, scary-looking villager approached the man and said he wanted to thank him.

A little worried, he followed the villager to a ruin of a hut, high on a hillside. This was his home. Once there, the villager offered him a chair and waved a hand to the sun setting on the distant horizon.

They watched, together, in silent awe and contemplation.

When the sun finally disappeared the villager lit a lamp and explained, "I had nothing else to give you."

A gift of beauty, a gift of wonder but, more importantly, a gift of something that also touches you deeply. Can you give a better gift in this world?

## Sunday — September 16

**NO** doubt prayer pleases God, but what does it do for the person praying? Mechthild of Magdeburg, a 13th-century Saxon lady, wrote that prayer "makes a sour heart sweet, a sad heart merry, a poor heart rich, a foolish heart wise, a timid heart courageous, a sick heart well, and a blind heart full of vision."

Really, when you think of it like that, it's a wonder more folk don't try it!

## Monday — September 17

**HOW** do you like being lost? The actress Marion Cotillard finds it exhilarating.

As a movie actor she doesn't always have the complete picture. Scenes will be shot out of sequence. Sometimes she will have no idea how what she is saying relates to the plot. But she can relax and enjoy the experience if she knows she is in the hands of a director that she trusts.

Life can be as confusing as an unedited movie. The question we have to ask is, do we have a director we can trust?

Sweet treats.

## Tuesday — September 18

I SAT with a friend talking about a hurt that had twisted his life. He had been upfront and honest. He told me that talking about it had helped and he was prepared to let it – and all its damage – go.

Then I asked him the most important question. Would he forgive?

His jaw tightened and he spoke not a word for a worryingly long time.

Eventually, I spoke again. "Will you think about it?"

"I will," he said. And I counted that a great victory.

## Wednesday — September 19

ONE of my regular walks takes me past a house big enough to have its own staff. I have often admired the beautiful gardens and one day I got talking to a retired gentleman who introduced himself as the Assistant Gardener.

Throughout the year I had complimented him on various floral arrangements. This time we fell to chatting just after he had planted the last of his autumn bulbs. And it occurred to me that he was the only one I had ever seen working in the garden.

"What on earth does the Head Gardener do?" I asked.

"Oh," he said, looking out over the ground he had lovingly prepared for winter, "he makes it all grow again in the spring."

## Thursday — September 20

ROSALIND RUSSELL had a long career in film and television. She played Rose in "Gypsy" and was His Girl Friday to Cary Grant. With her face regularly displayed on thirty-feet-tall silver screens, she would have taken great care to make sure her make-up was perfect.

From all those years of experience Ms Russell shared a tip we might all benefit from.

"Taking joy in life," she said, "is a woman's best cosmetic."

And, gentlemen, it might not make you prettier, but it will make your life more beautiful!

## Friday — September 21

THE great theologian Charles Spurgeon told of two men walking towards each other on a foggy night. The effects of fear and the fog convinced each man that the other was some sort of monster.

Cultural differences, accents, habit, skin colour . . . all of those things can take the place of the fog in Pastor Spurgeon's story. And it is often only in times of great trial or great joy, when all those superficial things are stripped away, that we realise we are all brothers and sisters.

## Saturday — September 22

SHE should have been enjoying her golden years. Instead, she found herself suddenly dependent on social services and the food-bank.

Making sure she had all she needed, I remarked on her cheerfulness. She told me she had lived a secluded life, afraid people would take advantage of her, and avoided company.

Now she was relying on strangers, living in a new place, and talking to new people every day.

"It's been wonderful," she explained. "All these years I never knew people could be so kind!"

I confess I was at a loss as to what to think when she left. I still am. But my life was lightened by the encounter.

## Sunday — September 23

IT'S difficult to imagine now, but the Salvation Army was once a new and controversial organisation. People often react badly to new initiatives and Catherine Booth, the co-founder of the Salvation Army, had her detractors.

Her response is one we might take on board even today when it seems the world is against us.

"Don't let controversy hurt your soul," she said. "Live near to God by prayer. Just fall down at His feet, open your very soul before Him, and throw yourself right into His arms."

## Monday — September 24

FOR my birthday a friend sent me a framed photo of some leaves! It was a close-up of a Japanese maple where it mixed with a hedge; the raspberry colour of the maple made a striking contrast to the yellow leaves of the hedge.

Now, I'm not the biggest fan of pictures of foliage, but I know the colours and their combination had meant a lot to him. He had nurtured both plants, never thinking they would go so well together, and had been delighted by how they did.

I have the photo on my wall now, on the understanding that he didn't send me a photo of leaves; he sent me his unexpected wonder and his understanding of beauty. Gifts well worth having!

## Tuesday — September 25

I VERY much doubt Englishman John Newton imagined his words "Amazing Grace" put to bagpipe music. But I'd guess that very few of us can listen to the hymn without waiting for the pipes to kick in. Two very different traditions joined to become much more than the sum of their parts.

If you are looking at something and thinking you might like to get involved, but you're hanging back because you don't think you're that kind of person . . . be the bagpipes!

If the thing itself is good and you approach it with a good heart, then the result might well be amazing!

## Wednesday — September 26

HARRY has some younger friends and relatives who, coincidentally, all seemed to have been having tough times recently. He helped where he could, but mostly they had to get through on their own resources.

I asked if it wasn't disheartening watching the young ones struggle like that.

"Not at all," he told me. "In the combination of their problems and their courage I see a lot of future wisdom and help for others being prepared. It is very reassuring!"

**Rainbow magic.**

*Callanish standing stones, Isle of Lewis.*

## Thursday — September 27

**S**OMETIMES you need to stand a good distance away from a problem before you can see it – and its solution – clearly.

How about 230,000 miles?

That's how far away astronaut Frank Borman and the crew of Apollo 8 were when they delivered their impassioned message to a troubled earth. Borman's personal prayer asked God for faith, love and wisdom. Then he ended by asking that each one of us be shown what we could do "to set forward the coming of the universal day of peace."

You and I don't have to go into space to ask that question, we just need to get out of bed with the notion in our hearts. And we will surely find some way to make our world a more peaceful place.

## Friday — September 28

**T**HE poet and hymn-writer Fanny Crosby told of a time when she was young and already achieving some success. Her friends were being very lavish with their praise.

She admits to a rising vanity that was nicely quashed by her superintendent. He called her into his office and said, "Fanny, I am sorry you have allowed yourself to be carried away by what others have said about your verses. True, you have written a number of poems of merit . . ."

There followed a silence in which she was sure he was going to be nasty and tell her she wasn't that much of a writer. Instead, he went another way.

He assured her that she was a good writer, but added she was a long, long way from the writer she might be with some real effort.

When we get to thinking we are wonderful, for whatever reason, we should ask ourselves if we already are all we will ever be. If we are, that depressing thought should curb any vanity. If we aren't, the thought of the work we still have to do should achieve the same effect.

Nicely done, Mr Superintendent!

## Saturday — September 29

HAVE you heard of the Fireside Poets?
In the early years of the United States a generation of American poets came to the attention of the public. The popularity of John Greenleaf Whittier, Oliver Wendell Holmes Snr and Henry Wadsworth Longfellow soon rivalled their British predecessors.

The group stuck to rhyming conventions and memorable, uplifting themes, making them family favourites and eminently suitable for reading out loud around the fireside. They were trusted.

How wonderful to live a "fireside" life! By that I don't mean a life spent with your feet in front of crackling, burning logs – although that would be nice, too. I mean a life that families would talk about and learn from whenever they gathered together.

## Sunday — September 30

COME with me a little while
Over the hills and far away,
Hitch a ride on passing clouds,
Forget the problems of the day.

See the mountains, tall and strong,
Through the ages, high and green,
Take their strength and capture peace
And deep within you'll feel serene.

Come away from noise and haste
And watch the tide flow in the bay,
Then with the seabirds travel far
Over the hills and far away.

Catch the sunbeams in your heart
And leave the troubled world behind,
Just now and then make time for you
And so recapture peace of mind.

– Iris Hesselden.

# October

DO you ever worry?
  I worry that you might. And I know that I do.

But I also know the 14th Dalai Lama gave good advice when he said, "If it can be solved there is no need to worry and if it can't be solved then worry is no use anyway."

But how do we stop?

Well, the great wit and writer Mark Twain had the following suggestion: "Drag your thoughts away from your troubles . . . by the ears, by the heels, or by any other way you can manage it!"

The idea of dragging them away by the ears might not cure our worries – but it will give us a good laugh, and that's half the battle!

*A BEAUTEOUS morning such as this*
*Inspires my heart, my soul, my all.*
*The risen sun is utter bliss;*
*Uplifting light, how can I fall?*
*A cloudless sky of topaz blue*
*Enthrals me as I raise my eyes,*
*And high my spirit flies to you*
*Oh, risen Lord who never dies.*
*The world awakes, another day*
*To start anew, refreshed and bright,*
*From dawn to eve, pray mark my way*
*And guard me through the darkest night.*
*As man and lark in bed and nest*
*Are stirring each from slumber deep,*
*Pray God revive their strength from rest*
*Oh, guardian who will never sleep!*

– George Hughes.

## Wednesday — October 3

HARP music played, a woman sang in Gaelic, dogs ran happily through long grass. The sky was blue, the air crisp. Two deer bounded towards the woods. That's how John described his morning to me. Sounds idyllic, doesn't it?

Asking more, I discovered that the dogs belonged to a sick neighbour. They'd been walking through a disused and overgrown industrial estate. The heavenly music came from an old mp3 player that was running out of charge.

The second version of the morning was the true one – but so was the first! The difference was in how John presented it.

How are you going to see your day today?

## Thursday — October 4

SCANS showed little Evie-Rose would be born with severe health problems. So seriously was it taken that a surgical plan had been drawn up for the first five years of her life.

And then she was born. And the problems were gone. Mum and Dad knew friends had been praying for her all over the world, but the doctors had no idea what had happened.

"Count your blessings," one offered by explanation.

"I do," Evie-Rose's daddy said. "And I also count my prayers."

## Friday — October 5

MARIE CURIE was talking science when she said, "Nothing is to be feared. It is only to be understood." Her work on radium and other radioactive substances greatly enhanced the understanding of the scientists who came after her.

I can't help applying the same maxim to people. Someone once said, "If we could know the secret history of our enemy it would break our hearts."

Understanding is the key to so much. And love, whether love of knowledge or of people, is the encouraging force behind it.

## Saturday — October 6

DO you have faith that things will work out, or do you hope they will?

Robert Louis Stevenson explained the difference – "Hope is the boy, a blind, headlong, pleasant fellow. Faith is the grave, experienced, yet smiling man. Hope lives on ignorance; open-eyed Faith is built upon knowledge of our life. Hope looks for unqualified success, but Faith counts certainly on failure and takes honourable defeat to be a form of victory. Hope is a pagan, but Faith grew up in Christian days, and early learned humility."

## Sunday — October 7

IN the early 20th century, Reverend John Henry Jowett wrote the following as part of a prayer – "We would thank Thee for all the bright things of life. Help us to see them and to count them and to remember them that our lives may flow in ceaseless praise."

You'll notice he didn't ask for more of those "bright things" – he asked that we might see them, implying that the bright things were already plentiful but we didn't always notice.

So, how do we see them? How do we get to that point of ceaseless praise? Paradoxically, we begin with praise. The more we appreciate what we have, the more we understand we have to appreciate.

No visit to the optician required!

## Monday — October 8

BEING a writer has helped Michael deal with his insecurities. Firstly, the writing itself is therapeutic. Secondly, he says that seeing a book of his go from a scribble on a page to a hardback volume on a bookshop shelf helped.

"We often compare ourselves to others and think we don't match up," he told me. "But we are comparing the rough draft of our thoughts and feelings to the finished product and shiny covers the others present to the world. As a writer, I can tell you there is an awful lot of editing goes on between the two!"

## Tuesday — October 9

WE were talking about the characteristics we most associated with family members, and Jean mentioned Auntie Sheila.

"She is the epitome of faith, the epitome of hope, and the epitome of charity." Then she told me a little of her auntie's story – and I had to agree.

Perhaps I shouldn't name her or everyone will want her for their auntie. When, actually, we should be trying to live lives that would earn us the same accolades!

But, Sheila Anderson, your niece Jean thinks you are the embodiment of the three graces. And it's no less than you deserve.

## Wednesday — October 10

OUR dear friend Mary was discussing career prospects with seventeen-year-old Eilidh.

"When I left school," Mary said, "the options were domestic service, factory work, shop work and getting married."

"Oh, it's very different now," Eilidh assured her. "These days anyone can be anything they choose to be!"

"Oh!" Mary said in pretend surprise. "Then I do hope more people choose to be kind!"

Good advice for any career choice, I think.

## Thursday — October 11

HOW do you face unpleasant tasks? I saw a street sweeper sigh over every piece of litter he gathered, and another street sweeper who made a game of brushing the pavement in front of an elderly lady, treating her like a queen.

Someone said, "If what you do is sweep the streets, do it in such a way that people walking in your neighbourhood say, this place was cleaned by a street sweeper who cared."

If you have to do unpleasant stuff, as we all have to from time to time, do it with a bit of style!

## Friday — October 12

**W**HILE her husband Mikhail concentrated on restructuring the Soviet Union, Raisa Gorbachev had other interests. Her take on youth warmed my heart, which perhaps speaks to the truth of the point she was making.

"Youth is," she said, "after all, just a moment. But it is the moment – the spark – that you carry always in your heart."

How is your spark doing?

## Saturday — October 13

**A** VISITOR to Jerusalem saw a rabbi walking past, followed by six disciples. The men were dressed alike, but there was more. Age had stooped the rabbi, so the disciples stooped themselves to be more like him.

It reminded me of a new puppy in a house where an older dog already lived. Within weeks the puppy walked like an old dog.

It's a wonderful thing to set a good example, but the example others follow might not be the one we want to set. A wise rabbi, or teacher, needs to watch out for that!

## Sunday — October 14

*H*E *was just a passing stranger, just a person walking by,*
*I hardly even saw him, so preoccupied was I,*
*Too busy in my garden – such a job and such a mess.*
*'Twas hardly worth my efforts, if my thoughts I must confess.*
*When suddenly this stranger stopped to pause beside by my gate.*
*He turned and, smiling, said to me. "Your garden's looking great."*
*So fleeting was the moment that he hardly did intrude.*
*But when I got back digging, well – how different my mood!*
*And better still, his action taught me never to delay:*
*Don't hang back with compliments – it might make someone's day!*

*– Maggie Ingall.*

Best of friends.

## Monday — October 15

IT was the first time he'd done anything like this. With two bags of hot chips in his hands, he sat down next to the homeless guy.

"Who are you?" the man asked, a little defensively. Darren told him his name.

"No, but who are you?" the man persisted. "Social services?"

"No," was the reply. "I'm just someone who cares."

"And that seemed to satisfy him," Darren told me.

As it should. "Someone who cares." I can think of no more honourable title.

## Tuesday — October 16

STUDY, diligence, good teaching; these will surely see you on your way to a decent education. You may learn many things down that route. But how much will you understand?

They say we only really understand another person by putting ourselves in their shoes. The Russian novelist Tolstoy expanded on that theme. "Anything I understood, I understood only because I loved!"

## Wednesday — October 17

SITTING through an orchestral performance, I found myself fascinated by how the percussionist handled the cymbals.

Sometimes he would bring them directly together, other times he seemed to control the vibrations by peeling the cymbals apart at greater or slower speeds.

I found myself thinking of how we speak to each other. You would think speech was a simple thing, like banging two metal circles together. But sometimes we need to have a tighter or looser grip on what we hope to achieve. We can prepare and present our words differently, and we can guide their effects with a little effort and finesse after we have spoken.

Crashes and bangs have their place, but if we are careful with our words we can always turn a noise into beautiful music.

## Thursday — October 18

TALKING of a mutual friend's desire to improve herself spiritually, the 17th-century monk Brother Lawrence said, "Our good sister seems to me full of good will, but she wants to go faster than Grace. One does not become holy all at once."

Life – all of it – is our classroom and we cannot know what the future would teach us, so we learn what today has to teach then we mull it over while we wait for tomorrow's lesson.

Always be graceful and always be learning about Grace. I can't think of a better way to live a life.

## Friday — October 19

HOW do you make a soul grow? You can't fertilise it, or water it, or position it in the place that gets the most sunshine. In fact, given that it is impossible to measure, a case might be made for the soul not growing at all.

But, in a letter to some schoolchildren, the great science fiction writer Kurt Vonnegut suggested a fun, if not proven, way to achieve just that.

"Practise any art," he wrote, "music, singing, acting, dancing, drawing, painting, sculpting, poetry . . . no matter how well or badly, not to get money and fame . . . but to find out what is inside you, to make your soul grow!"

## Saturday — October 20

IN 1790 a Suffolk landowner decided he wanted a better view. He took the cottages of his existing view and built a third one on to the other two. Then he built a tower on top of the third cottage so the whole building looked like a church.

The view may have satisfied his soul, but the building was still farm-workers' cottages.

The cottages/church remind us that it doesn't matter what we look like – or how hard we try to look like something else – it's what's on the inside that really matters.

## Sunday — October 21

THERE'S an empty frame in the Isabella Stewart Gardiner Museum in Massachussetts that asks some questions. One is, who stole the painting of Christ In The Storm? It has been missing since 1990.

In his only seascape Rembrandt depicted the disciples in a boat on the Sea of Galilee. A storm has taken them by surprise and everyone on board – except Jesus – is terrified. The question they have to ask is, do they trust in their own seamanship, or in Him?

Surprisingly, there is a thirteenth disciple in the boat. He looks very like Rembrandt and he is the only one looking out of the painting, as if to face the viewer.

His question? I don't know. I can only imagine it is, "What would you do?"

## Monday — October 22

GEORGE lives in a nice part of the country. But he has lived there all his life so far, and singularly failed to take it for granted! So much so that now he's retired he spends most days searching out new, beautiful aspects of it. When he posts the photos online they are regularly accompanied by the words, "Have you seen the place where I live?"

It is a lovely place, but a big part of the "magic" is George's enthusiasm; his determination really to see it, and keep seeing it.

With that in mind, I have to ask, have you seen the place where you live?

## Tuesday — October 23

ANGEL OAK tree in South Carolina (one of the warmer US states) is reputed to be 1,500 years old.

Amidst a list of fascinating statistics about the tree, I noticed that it produces shade that covers 17,200 square feet.

The older I get the more I understand that the whole purpose of being here is to be of service. It sounds like Angel Oak has that well and truly covered!

## Wednesday — October 24

THE schoolchildren brought their craft-work to give away at the care-home where Myra works.

She noticed there wasn't any common theme to the gifts. The pictures, sizes and textures, were all different. Then the teacher explained. The only instruction she had given the children was that whatever they made should make the person they gave it to want to smile.

Looking around at the happy faces, Myra was sure they had succeeded. But that simple instruction stayed with her. It's a rule we could all put to good use. Whatever we do, let's make sure it makes someone want to smile!

## Thursday — October 25

SIX men sat around the table. One, a rough-looking guy who looked at the end of his tether, finally confessed the secret that had shaped his life so negatively. There was a silence. Then one of the men said, "Same thing happened to me." Another man told his version of the same story.

The thing about secrets is that we keep them in the dark and they grow stronger there. Lay them out in the light, see them for what they really are, and take heart, strength and support from all the others who, like you, thought they were the only one.

## Friday — October 26

WE get used to living in a straight line. This job leads to that promotion, earns that income, buys that house. How much do we miss out in the rush to get ahead? What might we experience if we took the occasional detour, swerve or zig-zag?

I find my curiosity piqued by the unknown (to me) person who said, "I don't want to get to the end of my life and discover I have only lived the length of it. I want to live the breadth of it as well."

The straight-ahead life is all very fine – but let's take a look out to the sides every once in a while.

## Saturday — October 27

THE dog had barked the whole time I was in the shop. I saw his owner arrive and proceed to rant and yell at his poor pet for the noise it was making. A few feet away another owner quietly unhooked his well-behaved dog.

It was a real-life example of an old Native American tale. An old man tells his granddaughter he has two warring dogs in his soul. One represents hate and fear, the other love and kindness. "Which one wins?" the little girl asks. "The one I feed," the old man replies.

It bears thinking about, doesn't it?

## Sunday — October 28

THE bridegroom-to-be felt the wedding service really needed to be held in church to be authentic. The bride-to-be wanted a more open-air setting.

The minister settled it by assuring the man that the marriage would still take place in a sanctuary. It was just that the ceiling would be considerably higher.

If it's all God's Creation then every place is holy. Moses and Joshua were both on supposedly ordinary land when they were told the ground they stood on was holy.

This world we live in is a wonder and a blessing. And wherever we are in it – God is with us.

## Monday — October 29

IT started in Wisconsin. They have been seen in France, Germany and the Netherlands. Now they are firmly in the UK. Little Free Libraries might look like bird-boxes, some are converted telephone boxes – they come in all shapes and sizes. But they are full of books, free to take away and read.

The idea is to encourage literacy and bring neighbours together.

Todd Bol began it in memory of his mother, who loved reading stories to children. I am sure she would be delighted to see the good work Little Free Libraries are doing.

## Tuesday — October 30

UNCLE BERT told me of a man who, one day, quarrelled with everyone about nothing. Having told them all what he thought of them, he retired to his back garden.

In the stillness, he was aware of the time we have for happiness passing; in the vastness of the star-dusted sky he understood the insignificance of the things he had argued about; and in the silence he heard his better nature tell him the others were only human, with problems of their own, and perhaps none of his unhappiness was truly down to them.

Then he said thank you, although he didn't know whom he spoke to, but having someone to thank made him feel so much less alone.

Then he went indoors feeling like he was stepping into at least the possibility of a new life.

How Uncle Bert knew all that when there was no-one else in the garden but the man himself I cannot imagine . . .

## Wednesday — October 31

MOST of us are familiar with the Australian flag with the Union flag inserted next to the Southern Cross and above the Commonwealth Star. But would you recognise the Australian Coat of Arms?

It has an emu and a kangaroo on it. Both were discovered on that continent, but an Australian friend suggested there might be more to it.

He explained that both the emu and the kangaroo can cover ground rapidly when moving forwards, but have a more difficult time backing up.

His notion was that Australia, like the animals on its Coat of Arms, should always be striding forward.

Those of us prone to shilly-shallying or moving in circles might take inspiration from that notion.

Sometimes in life we have to move backwards but, as often as we can, let's make it the run-up to a great bound forward.

# November

## Thursday — November 1

GROWING up on the American frontier, Laura Ingalls Wilder knew better than most that so much of life is outwith the control of mere mortals.

Things happened for no apparent reason: wonderful things, dreadful things, completely random things . . . What can anyone be expected to do in such situations?

Well, in her opinion, born of experience, "It does not so much matter what happens. It is what one does when it happens that really counts."

Whatever the situation, resolve to make the best of it! It's what the Ingalls family always seemed to do. But isn't that what made the books Laura wrote so loved?

## Friday — November 2

SARAH was concerned about the time her grandchildren spent on the internet. Books were the thing, she insisted. Ten-year-old Sophie, who, despite being a computer addict, liked a good book, asked Granny Sarah what she'd read as a little girl.

Casting her mind back, Sarah recalled many happy hours lost in the words of L.M. Montgomery who wrote "Anne Of Green Gables". But Sarah's personal favourite was one she hadn't heard of since her copy got lost in a house move, "Emily Of New Moon."

A few days passed, then Sophie presented her granny with a surprise gift – a 1929 edition of "Emily Of New Moon"! Sophie's dad explained she'd bought it on eBay using his credit card, but she'd paid with her own pocket money.

A tearful Sarah is re-evaluating her opinion of the internet now. We both agree it's pretty amazing as it is, but with a kind heart like Sophie's behind it, well, it's just wonderful!

Autumn grandeur.

*Conwy Castle, Wales.*

## Saturday — November 3

IN 2009 Captain Sullenberger landed his disabled plane on the Hudson River; an incredibly difficult thing to do safely. When asked about it, he said, "For forty-two years I've been making small, regular deposits in this bank of experience, education and training. And on that day the balance was sufficient so that I could make a very large withdrawal."

The tough times you face in life, what you learn from them, and the skills you acquire to overcome them . . . they all add up. May you never have to make such a withdrawal. But if you do, may your credit, thanks to those tough times, be good!

## Sunday — November 4

WHY are we here? Books like Richard Dawkins's "The Selfish Gene" suggest the point of all of this is simply survival. J.B. Priestley had a more beautiful answer to the question.

"We are not here to multiply ourselves senselessly," he wrote, "but to increase knowledge, create beauty, and to increase love. Whatever helps to do these things is right; whatever stands in their way is wrong."

In this life, of course, we can never know for sure which answer is the right one. So, it comes down to personal choice. Survival? Or beauty and love? And of what use is the former without the latter?

## Monday — November 5

SOMEONE once said, "We tend to forget that happiness doesn't come as a result of getting something we don't have but rather from our recognising or appreciating something we do have."

Why not spend a little while today looking out for blessings you may not have noticed or that have been around for so long maybe you take them for granted? Take an old blessing out for some new appreciation. Or simply immerse yourself in an already familiar blessing until you have truly explored every bit of happiness it has to offer.

## Tuesday — November 6

PLANTS might well withstand the rain, the sun and the snow, but strong winds will scour a hillside, causing trees to bend in the direction they blow, if it allows them to grow at all.

The early 20th-century poet Charles Hanson Towne suggested that we might be similarly vulnerable – but there was a solution. Friendships!

"We do not really grow," he wrote, "unless we have friends surrounding us like a firm wall against the winds of the world."

And, of course, we each get to return the loving favour by being a brick in another friend's protective wall.

## Wednesday — November 7

THE Egyptian poet Salah Abdel Sabour wrote, "The poverty of the poor; the hunger of the hungry, in such eyes as theirs I see a glow which means something. Tell me, how can I close my eyes to the world and not wrong my own heart?"

It's a feeling most of us will recognise. We do the sensible thing – the thing our head tells us we ought to do – but our heart aches as we do it.

Whether or not we can turn away depends on whether we believe our truest self resides in the head or the heart.

## Thursday — November 8

THE Lebanese poet Kahlil Gibran once compared the heart to a tree. But, wait!

He said, "The heart's affections are divided, like the branches of a cedar tree. If the tree loses one strong branch it will suffer, but it does not die. It will pour all its vitality into the next branch so that it will grow and fill the empty space."

Some spaces will never be filled, of course, but we can always look for new ways to care, and given time, the heart will love again as much as it ever did.

## Friday — November 9

ELIE WIESEL, KBE, is a holocaust survivor, a writer and a Professor of Humanities. He has had to restart his life more than once, not least after being liberated from Auschwitz. So, he is well qualified to advise on the most important things when it comes to choosing your direction in life.

"First of all," he says, "you have to decide where you are going. Secondly, you need to know who will go with you."

Any journey is shorter, and more likely to succeed, if you make it with a friend.

## Saturday — November 10

SHOULD you be out without your crutches?" the woman shouted to her friend in the street. Her friend laughed and hobbled closer, leaning heavily on her husband's arm.

I couldn't help overhearing her reply as I walked by.

"Some folk need crutches," she said, "some have a stick, but I've got my John."

Her husband blushed, but a second later all three were laughing happily. As well they might! You see, it doesn't matter if it's a husband or wife, a neighbour or relative, or someone with a kind heart who happens to be in the right place at the right time. The humblest life is made immeasurably richer when you have someone in it you can lean on

## Sunday — November 11

SIEGFRIED SASSOON'S poem "Everyone Sang" tells of the moment World War I ended. He wrote, "Everyone suddenly burst out singing and . . . the singing will never be done!"

Sadly, it was not the end of war. Hymns of grief and regret have been sung too often since then. As we remember the fallen today, let us also sing a song of peace and encourage others to join in until everyone really is singing – dreaming of the time there is no need for any other kind of song.

## Monday — November 12

THE space around the war memorial has been built upon. Now it sits at the entrance to a shopping mall. On ordinary days, in good weather, children climb on its lower levels and people eat sandwiches there on their breaks. The bronze soldier atop it is hardly noticed.

With the poppies in place it was a more sombre scene. I asked an old soldier if he minded the normal "disrespect".

"A world where you can eat lunch where you like, where mothers can shop and children can play?" He nodded at the soldier. "What better could he have fought for?"

## Tuesday — November 13

THERE was a man who had worked at a business for the best part of a decade," he told me. "Then he did something really dumb and spent as long behind bars. After his release he found a letter on his doormat. It was from his previous employer and it said, 'The old place has space for a new man.'

"I've worked there for fifteen years now," he told me, "making twenty-five in total."

## Wednesday — November 14

I READ of a Welsh choir's friendly rivalry with a German choir from a similar mining background. The friendship fell away, as so much did, during World War II. Afterwards, when the world had time for such things as choral competitions again, things were different.

Many of the miners had been exempt from active service because coal was essential to the war effort, so most of them survived the war. But they found it difficult to relate to each other after all that had passed between their countries.

Then someone pointed to the words on the trophy they competed for. *Speak with me and you're my friend. Sing with me and you're my brother.* And they sang!

Oh, that all conflicts should be settled in such a way!

## Thursday — November 15

*WHEN daytime cares crowd in at night,*
*Be with us, Lord, we pray;*
*And let thy gracious strength of will*
*Take troubled thoughts away.*
*May healing strength be with us now;*
*The morning dawns anew*
*And problems seen in different light*
*Appear less daunting, too!*

– Elizabeth Gozney.

## Friday — November 16

ALEKSANDR SOLZHENITSYN, who spent years as a political prisoner, described the breath of freedom.

"I stand under an apple tree and I breathe. Words cannot describe the sweet fragrance that pervades the air. Inhaling as deeply as I can, the aroma invades my whole being. I breathe with my eyes open, I breathe with my eyes closed – I cannot say which gives me the greater pleasure!"

We all breathe. Why not try breathing as Solzhenitsyn did?

## Saturday — November 17

HENRY DAVID THOREAU built a hut on the edge of a pond and spent two years there, thinking and writing. But he was not always alone in that time.

He explained, "I had three chairs in my house; one for solitude and two for company."

Life is about balance, and too often we go too far one way or the other, spending all our time with others or all our time alone.

Socialise, by all means; relax, get to know folk, join in, help and be helped. But always keep a chair aside where you can spend some time just getting to know you.

## Sunday — November 18

**I**F we were preparing to talk to a celebrity, a politician or anyone we regarded as important, we would get ourselves together first. Wouldn't we?

God, by far the most important "person" we will ever talk to, doesn't require that. Teresa of Avila wrote, "Prayer is the way to open ourselves to God. He shows us our unstable hearts and begins to strengthen them."

We don't need to dress smartly, we don't need to have it all together – we just have to show up, with our unstable hearts.

## Monday — November 19

**I** TALKED with Chris, a brawler, a prisoner, a drinker. In passing, although he insisted it had nothing to do with his life, he mentioned that his father had never loved him.

I thought of him when I read these words by the missionary and writer Elisabeth Elliot – "There isn't a man or woman anywhere, I am convinced, who does not long for tenderness."

No matter how tough their defences, tenderness will find a way in and do its wonderful work. It eventually did with Chris. It turned his life around. Now he does talks in jails for other men who insist that they don't need tenderness, either. But he knows they do!

## Tuesday — November 20

**I** OFTEN hear about grumpy old men, though we rarely hear of grumpy old women. But you might think both sexes would have a way to go to be as happy as teenagers.

Actually, there is no competition. Teens aren't as carefree as we might think, and research by the University of Chicago suggests that, generally, we grow happier as we age.

Next time someone complains of aches and pains, saying, "Old age doesn't come alone," agree with them and say, "No, it brings happiness with it."

## Wednesday — November 21

THERE is no life into which a little "shade" does not fall. Thomas Jefferson, the third President of the United States, knew that only too well. There was shade and sunshine, good times and bad, in his life. Thankfully, he had friends to help him through. But he encouraged us all to remember that although some days may seem dark, "thanks to the benevolent order of things, the greater part of life is sunshine!"

Words to remember and believe when you find yourself in the shade!

## Thursday — November 22

THERE'S a path I've walked for years. One day I noticed it was quite overgrown. I kicked back the grass that had grown over the edges and discovered the path was twice the size it seemed.

I had known that once, but because the undergrowth moved slowly, summer by summer, I'd forgotten. Gradually, the path became less useful.

Bad habits do the same. They seem like nothing at the time but they work patiently, making us less and less use for anything good. That's why it's good to stop occasionally, kick back the undergrowth, and remind ourselves of all the good we really are!

## Friday — November 23

MEGA churches are mostly an American phenomenon, but they aren't confined to that country. When fewer people are attending churches they should be an encouraging sign. But critics point to the hungry that could be fed with the money it took to build them. I suppose the same could be said about the cathedrals of old. It's a dilemma for many. Do we serve God best by building things to His glory or by serving "the least of these"?

Rather than suggest an answer, I would like to offer this thought by the Dalai Lama. He suggested that "the purpose of all major religious traditions is not to construct big temples on the outside, but to create temples of goodness and compassion inside, in our hearts."

**Golden days.**

## Saturday — November 24

IT can be a wonderful thing to be swept away by some great event or movement. Exhilarating, and perhaps a little scary.

As the wife of Charles Lindbergh, the first man to fly solo across the Atlantic and a national hero, Anne Morrow Lindbergh knew that feeling.

We will never walk in her shoes, but she had an interesting take on the experience that we might share in.

"One can get just as much exultation," she said, "in losing oneself in a small thing as in a big thing. It is nice to think how one can be recklessly lost in a daisy."

## Sunday — November 25

*THE tapestry of friendship*
*Is sewn with threads so fine,*
*The gold threads and the silver threads –*
*Each of these intertwine.*
*Their pattern makes a picture*
*Which is truly rich and rare,*
*For the priceless gift of friendship*
*Is a wondrous thing to share.*

*– Helena Socha.*

## Monday — November 26

IN his science fiction novel "Out Of The Silent Planet", C.S. Lewis has his hero meet an angelic being who informs him, "My people have a law never to speak much of sizes or numbers to you. It makes you do reverence to nothings and pass by that which is really great."

"Out Of The Silent Planet" was published in 1938 and we still haven't got over the habit of thinking bigger is better.

The really great will come in all sorts of shapes and sizes – for those who aren't dazzled by numbers and expectations.

## Tuesday — November 27

HE described it to me as an idyllic scene. He was doing that soul-soothing thing of leaning on a gate in the countryside. The sky was blue, the meadow before him was splashed here and there with the colours of wildflowers. Wood-pigeons cooed, and a little girl of four or five years old played in the long grass.

Eventually, she wandered over to show him what she had found. In one hand she held a veritable bouquet. In the other hand she held a rusted fragment of an incendiary bomb.

"There was only one of these," she said, holding out her strange souvenir and sounding a little disappointed. Then she turned to the flowers. "But there were lots and lots of these."

It was the latter months of World War II, nearing the end of a time that would have tried anyone's optimism. But then, as when he told me the story, and as I share it with you now, the blessings always outnumber the bad stuff.

## Wednesday — November 28

MARY had written to her sister in Australia, faithfully, for decades, but eventually, and unexpectedly, the replies stopped coming.

After a while she mentioned her worries to her son, Eddie. He found an e-mail address for someone in his aunt's old neighbourhood. He found a name that might have been his cousin's child in a school newsletter. He e-mailed the Australian post office.

On Christmas Day Mary got a phone call from her niece, also called Mary. Her mum had been ill for quite a while, and that's why the letters went unanswered. The two chatted for an hour, then a delighted Mary called her son with the news.

"The miracle of the internet, eh?" Eddie laughed.

"Yes," Mary countered. "But don't forget the old neighbours who wrote to Mary, the school principal who phoned her up and the posties who tracked her through three changes of address. And you for looking."

The internet might be great at making connections, but it's still the human touch that connects heart to heart.

## Thursday — November 29

**S**AMUEL is a boy's boy; a three-year-old bundle of curiosity, mischief and energy. He is a handful at the best of times. Imagine what he was like at his birthday with all that added excitement.

Telling me about it, his mum sighed, adding, "Thank goodness there's only one of him!"

I'm sure she meant in her house, but her words are true on a grander scale. Despite a world population of over seven billion there is still only one of her son and one of everyone.

It's an impressive thought that we each get to add something unique, something only we can offer, into the mix.

Although some of those offerings, like Samuel's, for instance, might have to be chased, caught and tied down first before they can properly be appreciated!

## Friday — November 30

**T**ERESA OF AVILA wrote, "May your life become one of a glad and unending praise to the Lord as you journey through this world, and in the world that is to come."

It's a nice thought – so, let's think about it. Most of us are so busy getting by day to day that we don't stop to wonder what kind of picture, or story, our life would present as a whole. Would it be patchy, confusing, first this and then that?

Now compare that idea to how you would wish it to be seen.

Remember that under every masterpiece painting and great work of literature are early attempts, false starts and lots of corrections. And with that in mind, get editing or touching up.

You haven't been the only influence in your life, but you can emphasise or paint over the influences of others then fill in the spaces with as much beauty as you can gather together.

Ask yourself, how would you like your life to be seen? Now . . . go to work on that!

# December

ON this day in 1955, Rosa Parks was on her way to work in Montgomery, Alabama. She sat near the front in a segregated bus and refused to move to the back when told to do so. The result of the principled stance taken by Ms Parks and others was a year-long boycott on the buses by the black population.

Thousands of people walked to work day after day, costing the bus companies a fortune.

When the boycott ended, Reverend Martin Luther King Jnr knew the separated communities would need to get along together. So he issued guidelines for those people planning to take their place on the buses as equal citizens.

One suggestion stands out from all the others both in its degree of difficulty and in its potential to change the world. Bus riders facing aggression were advised to "Be loving enough to absorb evil and understanding enough to turn an enemy into a friend."

WHEN Billy Graham first "hit the big time" he was preaching the Gospel in a tent that held over 6,000 people. Every night when he preached the tent was filled to overflowing. No doubt great wonders were done in the big tent.

But there was also a little tent. It sat just beside the big tent. This was where Graham and his colleagues gathered for quiet prayer before each event, and it was often said that the real work was done there.

In the big tent Graham spoke to the people. In the little tent God spoke to Graham.

No matter what "arena" you do your daily work in, no matter what you achieve in public, make sure you have your own "little tent" (even if it is only the space at the foot of your bed) for the real work that everything else depends on to be done.

## Monday — December 3

A YOUNG friend of mine told me of a tree she found while on a long, rambling walk. At some point a swathe of bark had been stripped from it. The bark that was left thickened around the edges of the wound and the exposed wood gradually dried and split vertically in several places.

Someone had come along and painted the wound to look like a door, using the splits to give the effect of wooden planks. They painted a window at the top, fixed a mail-box to the trunk and a handle to the "door."

The worn path in the grass told her the three-feet-high door had plenty of visitors. The handle itself showed signs of wear.

I don't know which I find most amazing – that someone would turn damage into art like that, or that people would consider the fact that such a door might open, and possibly take them somewhere.

Either way, isn't it a wonderful world?

## Tuesday — December 4

M ISTER. Are you a minister?"
I said no and asked why he thought so.

"Because this is the kindest thing anybody's ever done for me!"

All I had I done was cross the road to pick him up, talked to him like a human being, and walked him home with his arm around my shoulder. He was very drunk.

Those of us who live comfortable lives tend to take kindness for granted. We forget that there are people whose lives involve precious little in the way of kindness; where hurt and harm are more to be expected. In their worlds a little kindness must seem a far brighter and much more precious thing.

The truth is, we have the opportunity to give out "diamonds" at little cost to ourselves. So, let us spread the wealth; that "wealth" being love, in the form of acts of kindness. Enrich another life, and enrich your own in the process.

But only if you don't mind being thought of as a minister!

## Wednesday — December 5

HAD a friend who knew a lot about the subject. Whatever the subject was. I never heard him say, "I don't know," or "Tell me more." He seemed a very secure guy, but his need to know was a hint of his insecurities.

A man who already knows learns little. So, fear of seeming ill-informed actually made him ill-informed.

On the other hand, if you approach each new situation from the point of view of knowing nothing and laying aside all you think you know, you will be amazed by how much you learn.

## Thursday — December 6

IN passing conversation, I mentioned Millport and Southampton. Harry remembered one as where he had fed a donkey and the other as where he had a bad fish supper. Amazingly, he has only been to each place once, as a child. Those memories had become for ever associated with the places despite each location having so much more to offer.

The majority of the people we meet in our lives we will meet once, usually in passing. Would it make a difference to the impression we wanted to make in those encounters if we thought the other person might remember it as long as Harry remembered the donkey and the fish supper?

## Friday — December 7

THEY are identical twins, in their forties. They dress in similar styles, but if I meet either one in the street I always know which it is.

They remind me of an old tale. A man, needing passage across a river, watched a group of horsemen ford it, before he asked the last rider for a lift. When the others asked why he had asked the last man and not them, he replied, "Because you all had 'no' faces, but he had a 'yes' face."

Only one of the twins has a "yes" face. It makes all the difference.

Wrap up warm!

*IF every card at Christmas*
*Was placed from end to end,*
*The love contained in all those thoughts*
*Would be enough to send*
*A loving balm, a healing,*
*To our poor, wounded earth,*
*And all the thoughts inside the cards,*
*Just think what they'd be worth!*
*It really would be priceless, the effort and the love,*
*If only all those messages could bring peace like a dove;*
*For using Love's great power*
*To link the hearts of men,*
*At Christmas peace would be restored*
*Upon the earth again.*

– Chrissy Greenslade.

## Sunday — December 9

THERE was a bit of an upset back in the early 1800s. Not that I remember it personally!

Isaac Watts and others were trying to come up with new songs to be sung in church alongside the traditional (and somewhat forced) musical renderings of the Psalms.

He didn't stray too far from the Psalms at first. He changed words to help them fit the music but tried to keep to the meaning of the verses, many of which were written by King David.

When he explained he was trying to put David's words and thoughts into a modern context, one detractor claimed Watts actually thought he was the great king. The hymns he wrote were called "whims" by people who thought they wouldn't last; hymns like "Joy To The World" and "When I Survey The Wondrous Cross".

In trying to understand the mind of a man who spent his life trying to draw closer to God, Watts created beautiful "whims" that outlasted both himself and his detractors.

## Monday — December 10

THE writer C.S. Lewis challenged us to imagine life as a building everyone lived in. But half the people thought the building was a prison and the other half thought it a hotel. The first group obviously thought it was intolerable, while the second group thought it really rather nice.

I have yet to discover a better example of the power of attitude and the difference it makes. We each get to decide if we are here against our will, or if we are actually honoured guests. The world will be the same, but the difference will be life-changing.

## Tuesday — December 11

RECENTLY I was in contact with a man in Iowa. A mutual friend had jokingly suggested she needed a fortnight on some paradise beach. The man replied that he already lived in heaven on earth.

I assumed he was referring to the movie "Field Of Dreams" where Shoeless Joe Jackson asks, "Is this heaven?" Kevin Costner's character replies, "No. It's Iowa."

"Never seen it," my Iowan friend responded.

It turns out there is really nothing special about where he lives – the wonder is in the way he sees that place.

Heaven is all around, if we have eyes to see it.

## Wednesday — December 12

SILSBURY HILL in Wiltshire is a colossal grass-covered, man-made mound. No-one knows why it was created but the effort involved must have been herculean.

Archaeologists reckon it was built to its original height of 20 feet with material brought in from elsewhere. The next 20 feet in height came from digging a massive ditch around it and adding the excavated material to the top of the mound.

Which goes to show there are always two ways of tackling any problem. You can build higher – or you can dig deeper!

## Thursday — December 13

THERE'S a man who bought a bunch of flowers to take to the cemetery for an anniversary. Between the flower shop and the gates of the cemetery, six different people asked him what he had done to upset his wife. Well, he was indignant!

"Can't a man buy flowers without having done something wrong?" he demanded of a friend.

"I don't know," the friend replied. "Can you?"

There was nothing left for him to do but prove the point. Now his wife gets flowers regularly. And she appreciates it. She hasn't told anyone that when he apologises he does so with chocolates!

## Friday — December 14

I FOLLOWED up on a long-held ambition recently and attended an art class. The instructor had an impressive body of work and we looked forward to a portfolio of tips. But my favourite came before we even put brush to paint.

"In still life," he said, "always remember to put your subject in the best possible light."

Walking home afterwards, I pondered his advice and wondered how different things would be if we looked to see the people we encounter on a daily basis in the best possible light.

As in still life so also in real life, perhaps?

## Saturday — December 15

MOST towns have a monument of one sort or another. But Enterprise, Alabama, has a monument to a beetle! It commemorates the time the boll weevil destroyed the town's only crop, leaving the residents facing financial ruin. Lest it should happen again the following year, the townsfolk diversified, planting new and different crops so that if one failed they would still have others.

Hard times often teach useful lessons, but how many of us erect monuments to them?

## Sunday — December 16

THE ladies were muttering disapprovingly, trying to outdo each other in indignation at the thought of someone like him reading the Bible.

The man on the bus smelled of drink and looked like he hadn't changed his clothes in weeks, but he was engrossed.

Ladies, it was surely written for him. You might want to reread the part where Noah gets drunk, the many parts where people are at their lowest and cry out for help . . . oh, and the bit about gossip is good, too!

## Monday — December 17

APPROACHING his ninetieth birthday, he said he judged his life not by its length but by its moments. Of course, astronaut Buzz Aldrin walked on the moon and in space. Those are pretty impressive moments. How does an ordinary life compete with that?

How about the moment you met someone who would change your life, the moment someone said they would spend their life with you, the moment you welcomed new life into the world, or kept company as someone left it? That first kiss! And whatever else you might like to add.

Ordinary lives might be just that, but they are not short of extraordinary moments.

## Tuesday — December 18

TIME and again I hear people extolling the physical and spiritual benefits of going out for a walk. And, I admit, I am a fan.

John Muir, the Scots-born American naturalist who helped set up that country's National Parks, once wrote, "I only went out for a walk, and finally decided to stay out until sundown. For going out, I found, was really going in."

Into your creativity, your peace of mind, the world, the universe; going in often begins with going out.

Ready for Santa.

## Wednesday — December 19

IT'S not an ancient tradition. The US is still a young country so ancient traditions are relatively scarce over there. But we might still learn from a more modern "tradition".

In the town of State College in Pennsylvania they have a midwinter festival called First Night. One of the many things the people partying there do is write a habit they would like to be rid of on a lolly stick (I told you it wasn't ancient), then they throw it on the bonfire and watch it go up in smoke.

How effective a remedy it is I can't say, but it does the most important thing when it comes to dealing with any problem. It identifies it.

So, this midwinter, or First Night, or New Year, why not spend a little time thinking about what we would like to leave behind with the old year? Then start a new tradition of our own; one that's better for not having that old habit in it!

## Thursday — December 20

THE story of the Christmas Truce during World War I, where the British and German soldiers sang songs, played football and showed off photographs of their family, is well known.

Less well known is the fact that they agreed always to stay a yard or two away from each other's trenches, preferring to meet in the middle ground.

Captain Armes, who was a part of that extraordinary event, wrote to his wife, "It did feel funny walking alone towards the enemy trenches to meet someone halfway, and then to arrange an Xmas peace. It will be a thing to remember all one's life."

And, of course, the world has remembered it ever since.

He didn't go all the way. He went halfway. His enemy met him there and, for a while, became his friend.

In honour of their bravery and the spirit of Christmas we might take a little walk towards someone we would rather be friends with. We need only go halfway. I am sure they will meet us there.

## Friday — December 21

IN the run-up to Christmas last year the local food bank started receiving donations of selection boxes as well as all the usual staples.

Then, one night after the place was closed, someone broke into the store room. They were looking for money and didn't find any. They obviously thought their hard work deserved a treat, though, because they stole maybe a dozen selection boxes.

The news of the break-in and what had been stolen hit the local papers a few days later and everyone was outraged.

But then something happened that was more powerful than outrage – the selection boxes started flooding in, along with tubs of sweets. Every child in every family who came to the food bank received an extra treat over the Christmas period.

And a local company, impressed by the good work that was being done, fitted a top-notch alarm system in the food bank for free!

Sure, there are people out there who will do bad things, even at Christmas. But never forget, there are infinitely more good people in the world and love beats hate all year round.

## Saturday — December 22

METHODS of writing have changed over the course of human history. Words of a sort might have been scratched on rock, or perhaps painted. Later they were carved. Then mankind learned to use clay tablets. Then came papyrus and the advent of ink. Chisels were replaced by quills, which were replaced by pens, which are currently being superseded by electronic gadgets.

But what of humanity itself? Have we changed as much?

Well, one of the oldest caches of handwritten messages was discovered in the north of England and is believed to be around 2,000 years old.

One of the "letters" was actually an invitation to a child's birthday party!

I am reassured that, however we write in another 2,000 years' time, the things we write about will still be pretty much the same.

## Sunday — December 23

SOME people take the idea of a prayer walk a little further. Instead of just walking the streets of their home town praying for the community, they knock on doors asking people if they have any needs the walkers might pray for.

It might seem odd. It might be a little annoying in the midst of your favourite programme, but beneath and beyond all that, isn't it a comfort to know that someone cares?

And someone always does!

## Monday — December 24

THE food bank doesn't distribute toys, but someone had donated a big and beautifully soft toy rabbit. They asked if I knew anyone who would like it.

I thought long and hard and a voice in my head kept reminding me of a women's refuge I had never visited before. So I turned up at their door, a stranger, just before Christmas, asking if they could rehome a toy rabbit.

The staff were lovely, but for the sake of confidentiality they wouldn't tell me if they had any residents at that moment, let alone the sort of little resident who might like soft toys. But they would take him in. So I handed Bunny Big-Ears (as I had named him) over in trust, and I left.

A few weeks later I had a note from the rabbit, via the refuge and the food bank. Bunny Big-Ears (who wrote very well with those big soft paws) wanted me to know he had made a friend immediately.

This little friend had left all her Christmas presents behind in her last place and so she had all the more love left for him; she took him everywhere with her, and now they would be moving on together to a place where rabbits and children could be safe and happy.

It seems my guiding voice knew exactly what it was doing when it sent me to that place.

It got me my first-ever letter from a rabbit – although I still can't read it without my eyes misting over.

## Tuesday — December 25

ELVIS sang "Why Can't Every Day Be Like Christmas?" Dale Evans Rogers, wife of Roy Rogers, suggested it could be.

"Christmas," she said, "is love in action. When you love someone you give to them as God gives to us. The greatest gift he ever gave was His son, sent in human form so that we might know what God the Father is really like. Every time we love, every time we give, it's Christmas."

It's good to have one day a year to remember what the others might be like.

## Wednesday — December 26

HARRY and I were walking home from a talk by a local artist. The man looks out for fallen trees in nearby woods, then he goes out with his chainsaw and chisels and carves them into long-boats, dragons, scenes of woodland animals, and so on.

And he leaves them there! The weather, the children and the occasional vandal do what they do, and the pieces he worked so hard on gradually decompose.

"Art should be like life," he said. "Life passes and so does my art."

"Well, really," Harry muttered on the way home. "All that effort. For nothing in the end. It's hardly worth it, is it?"

As he spoke I slipped on an icy puddle. I lurched sideways and might have hurt myself, but my friend caught me.

"In the end," I said when I was steady on my feet again, "your help will have been for nothing. But you did it anyway."

Beauty and kindness. If, ultimately, they are of no consequence in this world, I am sure they matter greatly to the next!

Of course, C.S. Lewis also had it right when he described the ephemeral things like friendship, love, philosophy and art as having no discernible "survival value".

Instead, he listed them among the wonderful, but transient, things that make survival worthwhile.

## Thursday — December 27

**M.A. BAIN,** a poet I would like to learn more about, wrote the lines, "Listen to the merry New Year's bells. All hearts rejoice and catch the cheerful tone!"

It's an undeniable fact (in my mind anyway) that there is something cheerful in the sound of carolling bells. Perhaps it is in the vibrations of steel against steel or bronze against bronze. Perhaps it has more to do with the enthusiasm of the bell-ringers. Regardless, there is joy in that sound.

Catch the cheer! And in the year ahead "ring" in such a way that others catch it from you.

## Friday — December 28

**JOHN MASON NEALE** was born 70 years after Isaac Watts died. But the former did not approve of the latter. You see, Watts was at the forefront of introducing new hymns to the church and Neale wanted a return to the traditional Psalms and songs.

And yet . . . these days we will happily sing Watts's "Joy to The World" alongside Neale's "Good King Wenceslas", enjoying both, and not thinking either one less traditional than the other.

History so often puts our disagreements into perspective. And what lesson might we draw from this? Perhaps, that if someone is adding beauty to the world we ought not to fall out over what type of beauty it is.

## Saturday — December 29

**THE** Indian poet and Nobel Prize winner Rabindranath Tagore said it was everywhere, in the earth's green covering of grass and the blue serenity of the sky, in the exuberance of spring and the absence of severe winter, in our living flesh, in the perfect poise of the human figure, in living, in the fight against evil, in the exercise of all our abilities, in acquiring knowledge, in working for gains we can never share.

But what was "it"? Nothing more, nor less, than joy!

## Sunday — December 30

*I'M fortunate to have a friend*
*As wonderful as you –*
*There's no-one who can make me laugh*
*In quite the way you do.*
*You're always there to listen*
*If I've something to confide;*
*You help me, in the troubled times,*
*To see a brighter side.*
*You know precisely what to say*
*And just how to advise;*
*It only takes a word from you*
*To make my spirits rise.*
*You're loyal and dependable,*
*The one I always trust –*
*I know you'll never breathe a word*
*Of anything discussed!*
*You're always understanding*
*Even if you don't agree . . .*
*My dearest, most beloved friend,*
*You mean the world to me.*

*– Emma Canning.*

## Monday — December 31

**I** TOOK the chance to ask people what the high points of the festive season were and a surprisingly common answer was "peace on Earth."

It's not that armies stopped going to war or anything. They meant things like a partied-out two-year-old being put into his car-seat and sighing, "That was great, Dad!" Or the brothers who hadn't talked for two years who shook hands at a family gathering. Or the moments all those mums sat down and put their feet up, glad it was all over and everyone was happy.

An end to war might be some way off, but until then we can be grateful for all those littler moments of peace on earth, at Christmas, New Year, and all through the next year.

Happy 2019, from the Lady of the House and myself. And may it be full of moments of peace.

**Moments to cherish.**